OXFORD EARLY CHRISTIAN TEXTS

*General Editor*
HENRY CHADWICK

━━━━

SEVERUS OF MINORCA

*Letter on the Conversion of the Jews*

# OXFORD EARLY CHRISTIAN TEXTS

The series provides reliable working texts of important early Christian writers in both Greek and Latin. Each volume contains an introduction, text, and select critical apparatus, with English translation *en face*, and brief explanatory references.

# SEVERUS OF MINORCA

## *Letter on the Conversion of the Jews*

EDITED AND TRANSLATED BY
SCOTT BRADBURY

CLARENDON PRESS · OXFORD
1996

Oxford University Press, Walton Street, Oxford OX2 6DP

Oxford New York

Athens Auckland Bangkok Bogota Bombay
Buenos Aires Calcutta Cape Town Dar es Salaam
Delhi Florence Hong Kong Istanbul Karachi
Kuala Lumpur Madras Madrid Melbourne
Mexico City Nairobi Paris Singapore
Taipei Tokyo Toronto

and associated companies in
Berlin Ibadan

Oxford is a trade mark of Oxford University Press

Published in the United States
by Oxford University Press Inc., New York

© Scott Bradbury 1996

British Library Cataloguing in Publication Data

Data available

Library of Congress Cataloging in Publication Data

Letter on the conversion of the Jews / Severus of Minorca;
edited and translated by Scott Bradbury.
(Oxford early Christian texts)
Includes bibliographical references and indexes.
English and Latin.
1. Severo, Bishop of Minorca, 5th cent.—Correspondence.
2. Bishops—Spain—Minorca—Correspondence—Early works to 1800.
3. Converts from Judaism—Spain—Minorca—Early works to 1800.
4. Judaism—Relations—Christianity—Early works to 1800.
5. Christianity and other religions—Judaism—Early works to 1800.
6. Minorca (Spain)—Religion—Early works to 1800. I. Bradbury,
Scott. II. Title. III. Series.
BR65.S393L47 1996 274.6'75202—dc20 96-33769
ISBN 0-19-826764-9

1 3 5 7 9 10 8 6 4 2

Typeset by Joshua Associates Limited, Oxford
Printed in Great Britain on acid-free paper by
Biddles Ltd., Guildford and King's Lynn

# ACKNOWLEDGEMENTS

A number of friends and colleagues read all or parts of this manuscript and offered helpful encouragement and advice. I owe a particular debt to two former teachers: Peter Brown, who introduced me to Severus' work at Berkeley in the early 1980's, and Peter Marshall, who offered expert advice on a number of problems of the text. I should also like to thank Howard Adelman, Karl Donfried, Justina Gregory, Robert Kaster, Ross Kraemer, Reyes Lazaro, Richard Lim, Carole Straw, Nicomedes Suarez-Arauz, and Robert Wilkin.

I am also grateful to Henry Chadwick for taking an interest in the manuscript and to Tom Chandler for his careful editing. My research assistant, Michelle Niles, was enormously helpful.

My wife's advice and encouragement were, as always, invaluable.

Northampton, Mass.
March 1996

# CONTENTS

# ABBREVIATIONS

| | |
|---|---|
| *AASS* | *Acta Sanctorum* |
| *AnalBoll* | *Analecta Bollandiana* |
| *ANRW* | H. Temporini *et al.* (ed.), *Aufstieg und Niedergang der römischen Welt* (Berlin, 1972– ) |
| *AugStud* | *Augustinian Studies* |
| BA | Bibliothèque augustinienne |
| *BAB* | *Académie royale de Belgique. Bulletin de la classe des lettres et des sciences morales et politiques* |
| *ByzStud* | *Byzantine Studies* |
| CCL | *Corpus Christianorum, series Latina* (Turnhout, 1953– ) |
| *ChHist* | *Church History* |
| *CIJ* i² | P. J.-B. Frey (ed.), *Corpus Inscriptionum Judaicarum: Jewish Inscriptions From the Third Century* BC *to the Seventh Century* AD, i², Prolegomenon to Second Edition by B. Lifshitz (New York, 1975) |
| CIL | *Corpus Inscriptionum Latinarum* (Berlin, 1863– ) |
| *CJ* | P. Krueger (ed.), *Codex Iustinianus, Corpus Iuris Civilis II*⁸ (Berlin, 1906) |
| *CRINT* | S. Safrai and M. Stern (edd.), *The Jewish People in the First Century*, Compendia Rerum Iudaicarum ad Novum Testamentum, 2 vols. (Philadelphia, 1974) |
| *CPhil* | *Classical Philology* |
| *CSEL* | *Corpus Scriptorum Ecclesiasticorum Latinorum* |
| *CTh* | Th. Mommsen (ed.), *Theodosiani Libri XVI cum constitutionibus Sirmondianis*² (Berlin, 1954) |
| *DHGE* | *Dictionnaire d'histoire et de géographie écclésiastiques*, ed. A. Baudrillart |
| *DOP* | *Dumbarton Oaks Papers* |
| *GCS* | *Die griechischen christlichen Schriftsteller der ersten Jahrhunderte* |

| | |
|---|---|
| *GRBS* | *Greek, Roman and Byzantine Studies* |
| *HJ* | *Historisches Jahrbuch* |
| *HTR* | *Harvard Theological Review* |
| *JEH* | *Journal of Ecclesiastical History* |
| *JIWE* | D. Noy (ed.), *Jewish Inscriptions of Western Europe*, i. *Italy (excluding the City of Rome), Spain and Gaul* (Cambridge, 1993). |
| *JQR* | *Jewish Quarterly Review* |
| *JRS* | *Journal of Roman Studies* |
| *JThS* | *Journal of Theological Studies* |
| *MGH AA* | *Monumenta Germaniae Historica; Auctores Antiquissimi* |
| *MGH SRM* | *Monumenta Germaniae Historica: Scriptores Rerum Merouingicarum* |
| *OLD* | *Oxford Latin Dictionary*, ed. P. G. W. Glare (Oxford, 1968–82) |
| *PG* | *Patrologia Graeca*, ed. J. P. Migne (Paris, 1857–66) |
| *PL* | *Patrologia Latina*, ed. J. P. Migne (Paris, 1844–64) |
| *PLRE* ii | J. R. Martindale *et al.* (edd.), *The Prosopography of the Later Roman Empire*, ii: AD 395–527 (Cambridge, 1980) |
| *PO* | *Patrologia Orientalis* |
| *RAC* | *Reallexikon für Antike und Christentum* |
| *RE* | A. Fr. von Pauly, rev. G. Wissowa, *et al.* (edd.), *Real-Encyclopädie der klassischen Altertumswissenschaft* (Stuttgart, 1894–1980) |
| *REA* | *Revue des Études Anciennes* |
| *REAug* | *Revue des Études Augustiniennes* |
| *REByz* | *Revue des Études Byzantines* |
| *REG* | *Revue des Études Grecques* |
| SC | Sources chrétiennes |
| *SDHI* | *Studia et Documenta Historiae et Iuris* |
| *ThZ* | *Theologische Zeitschrift* |
| *TLL* | *Thesaurus Linguae Latinae* (Leipzig, 1900– ) |
| *VChr* | *Vigiliae Christianae* |
| *ZKG* | *Zeitschrift für Kirchengeschichte* |

# SIGLA

**P**    *Palatinus-Latinus 856* (10th c.)
**W**    *Wolfenbüttel 2738* (12th c.)
**V**    *Vaticanus Latinus 1188* (15th c.)
**S**    *Saint Sépulcre 846* (11th c.)
**A**    *Saint Aubert 856* (13th c.)
**G**    *Saint Ghislain 3286* (11th c.)
**C**    *Charleville 117* (12th c.)

# INTRODUCTION

I. PREFACE

Severus of Minorca's *Letter on the Conversion of the Jews*, or
*Epistula Severi*, is a remarkable document that has received surprisingly little attention from historians. It describes the conversion of a Jewish community to Christianity on the island of
Minorca in February, AD 418, a conversion attributed by
Bishop Severus to the powerful presence of St Stephen the
Protomartyr, whose relics had recently been discovered in the
Holy Land and were just beginning to arrive in the West. The
arrival of Stephen's relics, alleges Severus, touched off a fire-
storm of religious fervour on Minorca. The previously cordial
relations between Jews and Christians deteriorated into an
atmosphere of mutual suspicion and distrust. Fearing violence,
the local Jews began to stockpile weapons in their synagogue
and to rouse their courage by recalling the example of the Maccabees, the famous martyrs of the Jewish past. In early February 418, this tension reached a climax when Bishop Severus
gathered his Christian congregations from both ends of the
island and challenged the Jewish leaders to public debate. The
distrustful synagogue leaders rejected the challenge, but
eventually agreed to let the Bishop inspect the synagogue for
weapons. The inspection, however, never took place. As
Christians and Jews made their way through the streets, a
stone-throwing riot broke out during which the Christian
crowd, after seizing the synagogue and removing its silver and
sacred scrolls, burned the building to the ground. For the
following eight days, this Christian throng remained in the
town and waged a campaign of scarcely veiled intimidation
until they brought about the conversion of the entire Jewish
community. According to Severus, 540 new converts were
added to his church.

Severus' letter thus stands at the confluence of two broad currents in the religious life of late antiquity: the rise of the cult of saints and the increasing intolerance of Catholic Christians against the unorthodox: pagans, heretics, and Jews. Tensions leading to occasional outbreaks of violence between Jews and Christians are known to us principally from the anti-Jewish polemic of the church fathers and from the Roman lawcodes. These sources certainly attest to the increasing willingness of orthodox Christians in the later fourth and fifth centuries to exert pressure on Jewish communities, but they tell us little or nothing about the local circumstances in which harmony between Jews and Christians broke down. Severus' letter is the only surviving narrative from the period that describes in detail the sudden collapse of social concord and the reaction of a frightened and disoriented Jewish minority as it faces the choice between baptism and possible death. Severus closes with an explicit exhortation to bishops around the Mediterranean to carry out the conversion of the Jews in their own communities. The *Epistula* is thus a central document in the history of religious coercion in late antiquity. It offers us an important perspective on the motives for religious intolerance, with its emphasis on the weakness of orthodoxy, the strength of society's religious outsiders, and the desperate remedies required to secure order in an age of upheaval. It reveals as well the tactics to which unscrupulous men could resort in this unsettled period in their attempts to undermine traditional patterns of authority and to usurp power for themselves.

It is important to stress that the *Epistula*, although transmitted with works on St Stephen, is not a hagiographical work in the traditional sense. It is fundamentally an anti-Jewish narrative and was circulated by Severus with a tract (now lost) containing anti-Jewish arguments for public debate. Furthermore, it has much to tell us about the life of diaspora Jews in the Western empire. Fergus Millar observed recently that the 'social, intellectual and religious history of the Jews in the Latin-speaking environment of the western half of the Later Roman Empire remains a largely unexplored field'.[1] The

---

[1] F. Millar, 'The Jews of the Graeco-Roman Diaspora between Paganism and Christianity, AD 312–438', in J. Lieu, J. North, and T. Rajak (edd.), *The Jews Among Pagans and Christians in the Roman Empire* (London, 1992), 99.

*Epistula Severi* emerges as a significant source for this largely unexplored field, since it preserves a wealth of detail about the social and religious life of a diaspora Jewish community, detail that is all the more welcome since Jewish communities in the Western empire are so poorly documented at this period.

The relative neglect of the *Epistula Severi* is due to a long-standing distrust of the work's authenticity and reliability, a distrust to be attributed in part to the nature of the work, in part to the circumstances of its publication. As we just noted, Severus' letter has come down to us with a group of hagiographical works describing the discovery of St Stephen's relics, their dissemination, and the miracles produced in their presence. Miracles and biblical typology figure prominently in the narrative, as in most hagiographical literature, so much so that many scholars dismissed the work as unreliable, while others suspected that it was the fabrication of a forger. Distrust of the *Epistula*'s authenticity has been exacerbated, however, by the defectiveness of the available texts. Most scholars continue to consult the work in one of the two versions of the text printed in the *Patrologia Latina*, both of which derive from the *editio princeps* published in 1594, and that original publication was based on the slipshod copying of a single manuscript in the Vatican Library. The texts printed in the *Patrologia* are riddled with errors, which have made a text that is already quite difficult even more obscure and thereby heightened scholarly scepticism about the work's reliability and authenticity. These doubts are largely unfounded. The *Epistula Severi* is demonstrably an authentic text of the early fifth century and its manuscript tradition is, in fact, quite good. Yet much work remains to be done on the letter, first, to elucidate its contents, and, second, to set it in the broader context of the social and religious life of the period. Many important issues in the work have never been investigated at all. I have presented my own interpretation of the *Epistula* at greater length and with fuller documentation in the Introduction, reserving the Notes for a brief commentary with frequent cross-referencing to the Introduction.

## II. DATE AND CONTENTS OF THE *EPISTULA SEVERI*

Severus dates the events of his letter with a precision that is rare by ancient standards. He claims that the drama on Minorca began 'on the fourth day before the Nones of February [= 2 February] by the power of our Lord Jesus Christ, and was completed eight days hence, in the year after the eleventh consulship of the Emperor Honorius and the second consulship of Constantius, a man of *clarissimus* rank' (31. 1). Honorius' eleventh consulship and Constantius' second consulship fell in 417, and the events recounted by Severus took place in the year *after* that consulship, hence 418. The use of a postconsular dating system should not trouble us; it was employed quite often from the fourth to the sixth centuries, usually early in the year when the consuls of the present year were still unknown.[2] Its use here thus helps us to determine not only the date of the letter's events, but also the date of composition, since Severus apparently did not yet know the consuls of 418. Pope Zosimus in Rome knew their names by 21 February, while the news had reached Ravenna by mid-March and North Africa sometime before 1 May,[3] but we cannot be certain when the news would have arrived on Minorca. The Spanish mainland was in upheaval at the time and communications were undoubtedly disrupted. None the less, Severus' postconsular date strongly suggests a date of composition soon after the events of the letter, probably in March–April 418.[4] In three different passages in the letter, Severus reports that the events he is describing took place over the span of eight days, hence from 2 to 9 February 418.[5] Moreover, the frequent use of time indicators within the body of the letter allows us to

---

[2] On the use of postconsular dating, see R. S. Bagnall, A. Cameron, S. R. Schwartz, et al. (edd.), *Consuls of the Later Roman Empire* (Atlanta, Ga., 1987), 65–6.

[3] Testimonia in Bagnall, *Consuls of the Later Roman Empire*, 370–1.

[4] A date of composition in early spring is probable, but not certain, since there are examples in which postconsular dates were employed by people who could have known and used the consular date if they had wished to make the effort, cf. Bagnall, *Consuls of the Later Roman Empire*, 65.

[5] Cf. 28. 1: *Sequenti igitur id est octava demum postquam veneramus die*; 29. 1: *Sane per hos octo quibus haec omnia gesta sunt dies*; 31. 1: *die quarto nonarum februariarum virtute Domini nostri Iesu Christi arrepta octo diebus ab eodem consummata esse.*

determine the following sequence of events with adequate, if not absolute, precision.[6]

*Autumn 416–Winter 418*: Severus explains that there are two towns on Minorca, situated at opposite ends of the island: Jamona facing west, Magona facing east. The bishop's seat is in Jamona, while all of the island's Jews live in Magona. Relations between individual Jews and Christians on the island had always been cordial, but the presence of so many Jews in Magona posed a problem, at least for Severus, who complains that 'Christ's church [was] being wounded by them daily.' However, the arrival of the Spanish priest Orosius and the deposition of some relics of St Stephen in the church at Magona produce a remarkable outbreak of religious zeal among the local Christians. By autumn 417, relations between Jews and Christians have become very tense. Only the social prestige of the Jewish notables of Magona, particularly Theodorus, head of the synagogue and *patronus* of the whole citizenry, has successfully fended off the threat from the local Christian congregation. Fearing physical violence, the Jews begin to gather weapons of all sorts in the synagogue, or so Severus alleges. The situation becomes particularly tense when Theodorus sails to Majorca to inspect an estate. Only his speedy return and the force of his personal authority (*auctoritas*) can quell, temporarily at least, the Christians' fervour. Eventually, the religious zeal that has fired the faithful of Magona seizes hold of Jamona and a critical decision is taken there. Bishop Severus plans to march his Christian flock from Jamona thirty miles across the island to lend assistance to the Christians in the neighbouring town.

In early January 418, there occur two dreams of particular importance in the narrative. Bishop Severus dreams that a noble Jewish widow sends him a letter in which she begs him to cultivate her untilled fields, since the sowing season is close at hand. The identical dream is also sent to a Christian nun

[6] The order of events is sufficiently clear, as are the two *termini*, but it is more difficult to assign events to specific days, since Severus uses phrases like 'after three days' (*post triduum*) without clarifying the initial day from which we should start counting. For similar chronologies, see G. Seguí Vidal, *La carta-encíclica del obispo Severo* (Palma de Majorca, 1937), 30–4; J. Amengual i Batle, *Els orígens del cristianisme a les Balears i el seu desenvolupament fins a l'època musulmana*, i (Majorca, 1991–2), 132–7.

named Theodora. Severus interprets the widow as the synagogue and infers that he is being called to sow the seed of the Word among the Jews and lead them to conversion. At about the same time, Theodorus, head of the Jewish community, dreams that twelve men stop him as he is about to enter the synagogue, warning him that a lion is inside. Although frightened and eager to flee, Theodorus peers into the building, only to see monks singing psalms with uncanny sweetness. The sight of the monks terrifies him, and he flees first to the house of a man named Reuben, and then to the house of a married kinswoman, who takes him to her breast and frees him from fear and danger. Severus claims that this dream is authentic and that Theodorus recounted it 'not only to Jews, but in particular to a certain kinswoman, a distinguished matriarch of that town, and to many Christians as well' (11. 2). Severus considers the symbolism of the dream to be perfectly clear. The lion is the 'Lion of the tribe of Judah, the Root of David' (Rev. 5: 5), which returns at key moments in the narrative, on each occasion terrifying the reluctant Jews and propelling them relentlessly onward towards conversion. Reuben will be the first Jew to convert and will offer counsel to Theodorus at a critical moment. His advice is prefigured in the dream when Theodorus seeks refuge with Reuben before finding a final haven in the arms of his kinswoman, a symbol of the Christian church.

2 *February*: The Christian congregation marches from Jamona on the western end of the island to Magona on the eastern end of the island. Severus dispatches clerics to announce his arrival and attempts to draw the Jewish leaders into a public debate. But they refuse, ostensibly because it is the Sabbath. Severus vehemently protests their uncooperativeness, arguing that he is not asking them to perform 'menial labour'. He wants their debate to be 'thoroughly calm', and insists that there be no 'stirring up quarrels, but rather a sharing of views in discussion'. After protracted and unsuccessful negotiations, he accuses the Jews of stockpiling weaponry in the synagogue with the intention of committing violence against Christians. They vigorously deny this accusation, even swearing an oath, and they are finally persuaded to allow Severus to inspect the synagogue. As Jews and Christians make their way through the

town, however, stones are hurled and a riot breaks out. The Christian crowd occupies the synagogue and, after seizing the silver and holy books, burns the building to the ground.

*3 February*: 'On the following day' (15. 1: *postera siquidem die*), Reuben becomes the first Jew to convert to Christianity. Since he is the first convert, Severus calls him the 'first-born' and likens him to Reuben, the 'first-born of Jacob' [Gen. 35: 23].

*4 February*: For three days (16. 1: *triduum, ni fallor, emensum est*) the Jewish community remains steadfast in its resistance. Finally, Jews and Christians gather at the site of the ruined synagogue. During a tumultuous public debate, Theodorus, the leader of the synagogue, loses control of his people when some of them mistakenly assume that he has decided to convert. Many Jews scatter in confusion, some seeking immediate acceptance in the church. While Theodorus is in a state of shock at this disastrous turn of events, he is approached by Reuben, who counsels him, if he wishes to remain 'safe and honored and wealthy', to imitate his own example and accept conversion. Theodorus ponders the advice and agrees to convert, but requests time so that he can bring all his people over with him. The Bishop accepts these terms and a wave of relief washes over the assembled Christians, many of whom run to embrace their Jewish *patronus*, confident that he will be able to persuade the entire synagogue to convert and thus avert the threat of communal violence.

Two Jewish notables, Meletius, the younger brother of Theodorus, and Innocentius, a refugee from the mainland, are among those who mistakenly believed that Theodorus had been coerced into apostasy. They have fled the public meeting and taken refuge in the hills. After a lengthy debate, they resolve to hide out on a farm belonging to Meletius and to emigrate when the opportunity presents itself, but *en route* to the farm, they lose their way in the rugged, unfamiliar terrain. Their courage falters and they eventually make their way back to town with the intention of converting.

*6 February*: 'After the third day' (19. 1: *post triduum*), Theodorus calls a public meeting of the Jews and suffers a revolt from those

Jews who refuse to wait any longer. Galilaeus, a young kinsman of Theodorus, and Caecilianus, who ranks second in the synagogue, both speak of the threat of Christian violence and proclaim their intention to convert immediately. Many Jews follow them to the church.

*7 February*: On the following day (21. 1: *sequenti igitur die*), Theodorus is reminded of his pledge to convert, but attempts to stall for time, fearing that his wife, who is on Majorca, will divorce him if he converts without consulting her. The Christians respect this concern, but the Jews who have already converted create such a disturbance that Theodorus risks losing all authority over his community unless he acts quickly. He and the whole Jewish community, as if a stumbling block has been removed, proceed together to the church outside Magona.

Artemisia, wife of Meletius, has remained alienated from her husband for two whole days (apparently since 5 February when he decided to convert). She and a few servants have been hiding out in a cave in the hills outside Magona. On the third day (24. 4: *ut primum tertia dies illuxit*), she experiences two miracles, returns to town, and accepts Christianity.

*8 February*: For nearly four days (27. 1: *per quattuor ferme dies*), the Christians have been trying to convert the wife of Innocentius, who had fled to the hills with Meletius on 5 February. Impervious to her husband's threats, prayers, and tears, she has firmly resisted conversion. At Innocentius' request, Severus and a throng of Christians have occupied his house in order to put pressure on his wife. After hours of fruitless entreaties, the Christians turn to the power of prayer, and after a long effort, Innocentius' wife agrees to accept Christ.

*9 February*: On the following day, that is, the eighth day from the journey from Jamona to Magona (28. 1: *Sequenti igitur id est octava demum postquam veneramus die*), Severus and his Christian flock decide to return to Jamona. Innocentius' sister-in-law, the only Jew to have chosen exile rather than baptism, returns from the open sea with her two children, falls at Severus' knees, and begs to be admitted into the church. In closing, Severus announces that 540 people were converted during the eight days in which the events of the letter occurred (29. 2). He rejoices that the 'land of the Jewish people, barren for so long, is producing manifold fruits of righteousness, now that the thorns of unbelief have been cut down and the seed of the Word implanted. ... For not only are the Jews bearing the expense, first, for levelling the very foundations of the synagogue, and then, for constructing a new basilica, but they even carry the stones on their own shoulders' (30. 1–2). Severus explicitly encourages his readers to 'take up Christ's zeal against the Jews, but to do so for the sake of their eternal salvation' (31. 2), that is, to imitate his own tactics as described in the letter.

## III. AUTHENTICITY OF THE *EPISTULA SEVERI*

After its initial publication by Cardinal Baronius in his *Annales Ecclesiastici* in 1594, roughly a century and a half passed before the *Epistula Severi* was subjected to its first scholarly scrutiny by L. du Mesnil in *Doctrina et Disciplina Ecclesiae*, published in Venice in 1752. Du Mesnil's reaction was symptomatic of the attitude of many later scholars. Disdain for the letter's miracles led him to dismiss the entire narrative as ultimately of little use for the historian.[7] In the nearly two and a half centuries since Du Mesnil first voiced his scepticism, a number of important scholars have expressed similar reservations, dismissing Severus' narrative as a wilful distortion or even an outright forgery.[8] Standard reference works, even of recent publication, often voice doubt about the authenticity of the letter.[9]

[7] L. Du Mesnil, *Doctrina et Disciplina Ecclesiae*, ii (Venice, 1752), 284: 'putamus interpolatam [epistulam] pluribus factis extraordinariis et miraculis inter se male consutis.'

[8] M. Kayserling, *Geschichte der Juden in Spanien und Portugal*, i (Berlin, 1861), 156–8 considered it obvious that the narrative had been so distorted and falsified that it was not possible to determine what had actually happened on Minorca. Similarly, H. Graetz, in his ten-volume *Geschichte der Juden*, published from 1853 onward and translated into several languages, accorded only a cursory summary to Severus' epistle, which he considered a wilful distortion, if not an outright fabrication, cf. *Geschichte der Juden*, iv (Leipzig, 1908), 361: 'dem geflissentlich entstellten, wenn nicht gar erdichteten Sendschreiben'. Expressions of doubt, as opposed to blunt condemnation, are frequently encountered, e.g. Z. García Villada, *Historia Eclesiástica de España*, i (Madrid, 1929), 262: 'unas letras encíclicas, de autenticidad algo sospechosa'.

[9] e.g. E. Hübner, *RE* 2. 2827: 'der Brief des Bischofs von Menorca Severus,

The most significant critic, however, was Bernhard Blumenkranz, who, in numerous publications on Jewish–Christian
relations in the late Roman and early medieval periods, invariably treated the *Epistula Severi* as a forgery. Blumenkranz's
reservations must be treated in some detail, since they more
than any other factor have prevented the work from receiving
the attention it deserves. Blumenkranz recognized the importance of the letter and often cited it, but he did not regard it as
an authentic document of the fifth century. In an important
survey of medieval Christian writers on Jews and Judaism, he
catalogued Severus as '(Ps.-) Sévère de Minorque (VII<sup>e</sup> siècle)'
and set out his reservations about authenticity, which he then
repeated in subsequent publications, usually in footnotes,
whenever he had occasion to use the letter.[10] His arguments
were as follows: (1) an *argumentum ex silentio*, in this instance,
the silence of Severus' contemporaries concerning the miraculous conversion of Minorca's Jews. In his view, Augustine's
failure to mention this remarkable event was particularly
damning, and he found it incredible that some scholars could
accept so uncritically the historicity of the work.[11] (2) Severus
mentions having attached to his encyclical letter an anti-Jewish
tract (*commonitorium*). This detail, argued Blumenkranz, recalls
Canon IX of the Twelfth Council of Toledo (AD 681), which
enjoined Catholic bishops to compose a tract (*libellum*) for their
local Jews in order to set forth their errors and to refute them.[12]
(3) A linguistic peculiarity demonstrates that the document

angeblich aus dem J. 418 . . . er ist aber sicher weit jüngeren Ursprungs'; D. Lambert,
*DHGE* 6. 368: 'Une pièce condamnée par bon nombre d'érudits de nos jours, mais qui
remonte certainement à une très haute antiquité, en dépit de quelques expressions
vraiment inquiétantes, la *Epistola Severi*'; E. Romero Pose, *Encyclopedia of the Early
Church* (New York, 1992, orig. publ. in Italian, 1982), *s.v.* Severus of Minorca. Romero
Pose's 'balanced' and non-committal treatment conveys the impression that the work is
untrustworthy.

[10] Cf. 'Les Auteurs chrétiens latins du moyen âge sur les juifs et le judaïsme', *REJ* 11
[111] (1951–2), 24 n. 3, for Blumenkranz's claim that he would treat at length the
letter's authenticity in an article to appear in *Revue du moyen âge latin*. However, the long
article that soon appeared, 'Altercatio Aecclesie contra Synagogam. Texte inédit du X<sup>e</sup>
siècle', *Revue du moyen âge latin* 10 (1954), 1–159, mentioned the *Epistula Severi*, but did
not elaborate on the problem of authenticity. The instalments of the survey entitled
'Les Auteurs chrétiens latins . . .' published in *Revue des études juives* were later collected
and published as a single volume, *Les auteurs chrétiens latins du moyen âge sur les juifs et le
judaïsme* (Paris, 1963), with no addition regarding the authenticity of the *Ep. Sev.*

[11] B. Blumenkranz, *Die Judenpredigt Augustins* (Paris, 1946), 57–8.

[12] Blumenkranz, 'Les Auteurs chrétiens latins' 25 n. 5.

could not possibly have been written in 418. At a critical moment in the narrative, after the failure of all attempts to persuade the head of the synagogue, Theodorus, to convert, the Christian throng cries out in unison, 'Theodorus, believe in Christ!' (*Theodore, credas in Christum!*). Panic strikes the Jews when, in the mêlée, they understand the Christians to be shouting, 'Theodorus believes in Christ!' (*Theodorus in Christum credidit!*). Such a linguistic confusion was possible in Spanish, but not in Latin, which suggests that the text was composed after the transition to the Romance language had begun.[13] (4) Severus' elaborate salutation with its detailed enumeration of the church hierarchy ('Lord Bishops, Presbyters, Deacons, and the Universal Brethren of the Whole World') is unattested in a letter, as opposed to other church documents, before 649.[14]

As part of his argument against authenticity, Blumenkranz offered a hypothesis about the *Epistula Severi*'s origin, supplying an appropriate context and motivation for what historical instinct told him was a literary fake. The atmosphere of physical intimidation so conspicuous in the letter seemed to him to fit perfectly a seventh-century Spanish context, but seemed out of place in the early fifth century. In seventh-century Spain, churchmen debated vigorously whether gentle persuasion or strong-arm tactics were more likely to produce conversions. Moreover, the seventh century was a period in which literary forgery was fairly common. Blumenkranz hypothesized that the *Epistula Severi* fitted well into this historical context and would have been forged in order to provide an 'ancient' historical precedent for those who advocated physical coercion of Jews.[15]

When Blumenkranz's reservations are collected and set forth together, their weakness becomes readily apparent. None of these arguments is compelling, and Blumenkranz said nothing about the strong arguments in favour of authenticity. As we noted above, it is rare for an ancient document to be dated so

[13] Ibid. 26 n. 1.
[14] Ibid. 24 n. 4.
[15] B. Blumenkranz, 'Die jüdischen Beweisgründe im Religionsgespräch mit den Christen in den christlich-lateinischen Sonderschriften des 5. bis 11. Jahrhunderts', *ThZ* 4 (1948), 128–9 (reprinted in id., *Juifs et chrétiens, patristique et moyen âge* (London, 1977), xix). He repeated this point in later works: id., 'Les Auteurs chrétiens latins' 24–5; id., *Juifs et chrétiens dans le monde occidental 430–1096* (Paris, 1960), 76 n. 34.

precisely (cf. 31. 1). In an earlier chapter (12. 4), Severus had
mentioned that the day of his arrival in Magona, 2 February,
was a Sabbath. That detail is accurate, since 2 February 418
was, in fact, a Saturday.[16] At 29. 1, he mentions that the events
of the letter occurred before the beginning of Lent. That detail
too is correct, since the first Sunday of Lent fell on 24 February
in 418, whereas in 417 it fell on 4 February.[17] No seventh-
century forger would know these facts. Moreover, the most
significant of his arguments, the argument from silence, is
simply a mistake, since two contemporaries do allude to
Bishop Severus and to the miraculous events on Minorca. One
of these references only came to light after Blumenkranz had
published his work, but the other reference has been known
and duly cited in every edition of the *Epistula Severi* since its
original publication by Baronius in 1594. But first, let us
examine Blumenkranz's objections on more technical points.[18]
Severus' use of the word *commonitorium* for an anti-Jewish tract
can hardly be considered unusual. The word occurs frequently
in the titles of religious tracts in this period, as, for example, in
Orosius' *Commonitorium de errore Priscillianistarum et Origenistarum*, and Severus' contemporary, Consentius, who also lived
in the Balearics, uses the same word of his own religious
pamphlets or memoranda.[19] Second, the elaborate salutation
to the church hierarchy poses no problem, since parallels are
ready to hand.[20] Third, in his references to the linguistic con-

---

[16] Noted by J. Wankenne and B. Hambenne, 'La Lettre-encyclique de Severus
évêque de Minorque au début du Vᵉ siècle', *Revue bénédictine*, 97 (1987), 18.
[17] Noted by E. Demougeot, 'L'Évêque Sévère et les juifs de Minorque au Vᵉ siècle',
in *Majorque, Languedoc et Roussillon de l'Antiquité à nos jours*, Actes du IIIᵉ congrès de la
féderation historique du Languedoc méditerraneen et du Roussillon, Palma de
Mallorca, 16–17 mai 1980 (Montpellier, 1982), 16 n. 3.
[18] Blumenkranz's arguments have also been reviewed and critiqued by M. Sotomayor y Muro, *Historia de la Iglesia en España*, i: *La iglesia en la España romana y visigoda*
(Madrid, 1979), 355–9; Amengual i Batle, *Els orígens del cristianisme*, i. 66–72.
[19] Consentius' letter is found at Aug. *Ep.* 11*. 2. 1: *litteras et commonitoria et libros quos
transmiseras repperi*; 10. 3: *'Ubi', inquit, 'sunt Consentii epistolae et commonitoria illa nescio
quae . . . ?'*. These *commonitoria* are memoranda or compendia of religious arguments,
written out by Consentius to assist the monk Fronto in undercover operations against
Priscillianists in Tarragona.
[20] Cf. Eusebius, *HE* 7. 30. 2 (on the heresy of Paul of Samosata, sent in 269): Διονυ-
σίῳ καὶ Μαξίμῳ καὶ τοῖς κατὰ τὴν οἰκουμένην πᾶσιν συλλειτουργοῖς ἡμῶν ἐπισκόποις
καὶ πρεσβυτέροις καὶ διακόνοις καὶ πασῃ τῇ ὑπὸ τὸν οὐρανὸν καθολικῇ ἐκκλησίᾳ. More
importantly, Blumenkranz failed to notice that Severus is imitating (and conflating) the
styles of two letters which figure prominently in the dossier on Stephen, the *Epistula*

fusion, the argument repeated most frequently, he apparently had in mind that the present imperative (*cree*) and the present indicative (*cree*) are identical in Spanish, but Severus uses a present subjunctive (*credas*) and a perfect indicative (*credidit*). In any event, the interpretation is the result of an overly literal reading of the scene, which involves the first public debate between the Bishop and the head of the synagogue since a stone-throwing riot two days previously, when the Christians had burned the synagogue to the ground. The atmosphere is extremely tense and degenerates into a shouting match in which some of the Jews, who rightly fear violence, mistakenly hear that the head of the synagogue, Theodorus, has agreed to convert. The result is panic and a general flight from the public square. At this critical moment, as at other critical moments in the narrative, Severus invokes the miraculous. Where human persuasion fails, the power of Christ triumphs. The scene tells us nothing about the formation of the Romance languages.

More significant is the argument based on the silence of contemporaries. Blumenkranz failed to account for a specific reference to Severus' letter in the *De Miraculis Sancti Stephani*, a collection of Stephen's miracles composed *c*.425 in Uzalis. Migne himself found this confirmation of authenticity in Baronius's *Annales Ecclesiastici* and noted it in both versions of the text he printed.[21] In *De Miraculis* 1. 2, the author alludes to the remarkable events that had occurred on Minorca in February 418:

On the same day on which the relics of the blessed Stephen entered the church, at the very beginning of the Scripture reading, a letter was delivered to us from a certain holy bishop, Severus by name, from the island of Minorca, and was read from the pulpit for the ears of the church to the accompaniment of great applause. It contained the marvellous deeds of the

*Aviti* and the *Revelatio Sancti Stephani*, both of which Orosius was carrying when he visited Minorca and both of which he clearly showed to Severus (see below pp. 23–4). Cf. *Ep. Aviti* 1: *Beatissimo dilectissimoque semper in Domino Papae Balconio atque universo clero et plebi ecclesiae Bracarensis, Avitus presbyter in Domino aeternam salutem*; *Rev.* A, 1: *Lucianus misericordia indigens et omnium hominum minimus, presbyter ecclesiae Dei quae est in villa Caphargamala in territorio Hierosolymorum, sanctae ecclesiae omnibus sanctis qui sunt in Christo Iesu in universo mundo, in Domino salutem.*

[21] Cf. *PL* 20. 746; 41. 821.

glorious Stephen, which he had accomplished on that island through the presence of his relics for the salvation of all the Jews there who believed.

*Eodem namque die in quo ingressae sunt ecclesiam beati Stephani reliquiae, in ipso principio canonicarum lectionum, epistola ad nos quoque delata cuiusdam sancti episcopi, Severi nomine, Minoricensis insulae, de pulpito in aures ecclesiae cum ingenti favore recitata est; quae continebat gloriosi Stephani virtutes, quas in insula memorata per praesentiam reliquiarum suarum in salutem omnium illic credentium perfecerat Iudaeorum.*[22]

The author alludes here to an *adventus* ceremony that had taken place at least seven years previously. Stephen's relics, he implies, were received in the basilica at Uzalis on the very day when Severus' letter describing events on Minorca in February 418 arrived.[23]

---

[22] *PL* 41. 835. Aug. *De Civ. Dei* 22. 8, composed *c*.425/6, argues that miracles are still performed at the present day and recounts a series of healing tales, many of which involve shrines of Stephen and some of which mention the presence of his relics. But, complains Augustine, people do not publish accounts of the miraculous events that do occur. Consequently, he has himself begun to encourage people to compose narratives of miraculous events to be disseminated and recited in the presence of the faithful (*CSEL* 40(2). 607). Stephen's relics, for example, had arrived in Hippo only two years before (*c*.423), but there were now in circulation seventy *libelli* describing miracles worked in their presence (607–8). The relics had arrived at Uzalis long before they arrived in Hippo, but in Augustine's words, 'there the custom of publishing narratives (*libelli*) does not obtain, or, I should say, did not obtain, for possibly it may now have been begun' (608). He then informs us that on a recent visit to Uzalis, he had, with Evodius' permission, encouraged a noblewoman, Petronia, to compose an account of a miraculous cure that she had experienced (608). The *De Miraculis Sancti Stephani*, containing miracles performed by Stephen at Uzalis, was composed at the bidding of Evodius by an unknown author, presumably one of his clergymen. In light of what Augustine says about the previous lack of such *libelli* at Uzalis, it is likely that the *De Miraculis Sancti Stephani* was composed soon after 425.

[23] The evidence of the *De Miraculis* would appear to offer positive proof of the authenticity of the *Ep. Sev.*, but this evidence too has been questioned. Cf. M. C. Díaz y Díaz, 'De patrística española', *Revista Española de teología*, 17 (1957), 11 n. 30, who reviewed Blumenkranz's arguments and concluded that no firm conclusions about authenticity could be reached. But Díaz y Díaz was also sceptical and added his own hesitations about authenticity, pointing out that the work is invariably transmitted in the manuscript tradition with the *De Miraculis*. He offered the hypothesis that the mention of Severus' letter in the *De Miraculis* was either an interpolation or that the *Ep. Sev.* was itself a forgery based on the mention in the *De Miraculis* of a letter from a Bishop Severus. Seguí Vidal, *La carta-encíclica*, 25–6, 35–8 had already provided an adequate explanation for the fact that the *Ep. Sev.* and the *De Miraculis* are transmitted together in the manuscript tradition. He hypothesized that our manuscript tradition of the *Ep. Sev.* derives ultimately from Uzalis. Evodius, he noted, had received Severus'

The discovery over a decade ago of two new manuscripts of St Augustine's letters has corroborated the evidence of the *De Miraculis*. In the corpus of letters published in 1981 by Johannes Divjak stand two epistles, 11\* and 12\*, composed by a Consentius, who lived in the Balearic Islands, and who is known from Augustine's *Epp*. 119–120 and 205. In *Ep*. 12\*, addressed to Augustine and probably composed in 419, Consentius alludes to the miraculous events that had recently taken place on Minorca and to Bishop Severus' intention of composing a narrative letter about them:

It happened at that same time that certain miraculous things were performed among us at the bidding of the Lord. When the blessed priest, the brother of your Paternity, Bishop Severus, along with others who had been present, had recounted these things to me, by the great force of his love he broke down my resolution [*viz*. not to engage in literary composition] and he borrowed from me some words and phrases— but no more than that—in order that he himself might write a letter containing a narrative of the events.

*Eodem tempore accidit, ut quaedam apud nos ex praecepto domini mirabilia gererentur. Quae cum mihi beatus antistes, frater paternitatis tuae Severus episcopus cum ceteris qui affuerant rettulisset, irrupit propositum meum summis viribus caritatis et, ut epistolam quae rei gestae ordinem contineret ipse conscriberet, sola a me verba mutuatus est.*[24]

The passage offers independent confirmation that the *Epistula Severi* is exactly what it claims to be: an encyclical letter composed by Severus, Bishop of Minorca, in 418 to describe the conversion of the island's Jews.

---

letter and the man who composed the *De Miraculis* clearly imitated Severus' letter, since both works open with an unusual reference to the Book of Tobit. These works are usually transmitted together, often with other works concerning the cult of Stephen, and probably ultimately derive from North Africa.

[24] *Ep*. 12\*. 13. 5–6.

## IV. ST STEPHEN, THE DISCOVERY OF HIS RELICS, AND THE VOYAGE TO MINORCA

Despite his status as the Protomartyr, Stephen was not the object of any special veneration in the early church, nor did he serve as a focal point of anti-Jewish polemic among the early Christians.[25] The location of Stephen's burial, moreover, remained a mystery for nearly four hundred years. In December 415, however, it was revealed in waking visions to a certain Lucian, priest of the church on an estate called Kefar Gamala north of Jerusalem. We know the circumstances of the recovery of the relics from Lucian's own account entitled the *Revelatio Sancti Stephani*, or more commonly, the *Epistula Luciani*.[26] This work proved very popular in the Greek East and survives in many versions: three in Greek, two in Syriac, and one each in Armenian, Georgian, and Ethiopian. The recovery of the relics also prompted the composition of a *Passion of St Stephen*, based in part on the account in Acts 6–7, but treating themes relevant to the concerns of Christians in the fifth century.[27] The *Passion* was clearly composed sometime after the revelation of Stephen's relics in 415, since Stephen predicts their discovery in the *Passion*, and apparently before the mid-fifth century, since the author shows considerable interest in Mary's status as Theotokos, 'god-bearer', a title much discussed in the first half of the fifth century.[28] Although the *Passion* does not survive in Greek or Latin, it is preserved in several Georgian manuscripts along with the Georgian version of the *Revelatio Sancti Stephani*. The *Passion* and the *Revelatio* are thus closely linked in theme and both works may have been composed, as Michel van Esbroeck suggested, with the encouragement of Bishop John of Jerusalem, who presided over the discovery and dissemination of Stephen's relics.[29]

---

[25] On Stephen's legacy, see M. Simon, *St. Stephen and the Hellenists in the Primitive Church* (London, 1958), 98–116.

[26] Published in *PL* 41. 807–18 with the title *Epistula Luciani*.

[27] The *Passion* is translated by M. van Esbroeck, 'Jean II de Jérusalem et les cultes de S. Étienne, de la Sainte-Sion et de la Croix', *AnalBoll* 102 (1984), 101–5.

[28] *Passion* 2, 4 (references to the Theotokos); 10 (prediction of the discovery of the relics).

[29] Van Esbroeck, 'Jean II de Jérusalem' 100 suggests that John's political initiatives may lie behind the composition of both the *Passion* and the *Revelatio*.

Stephen's prediction in the *Passion* that his relics would eventually be recovered is obviously linked to Lucian's *Revelatio Sancti Stephani*, which Lucian apparently dictated in Greek to the bilingual Avitus of Braga, who took down the account in Greek, but immediately translated it into Latin and augmented it with a few additions. Avitus' Latin translation is, in effect, an original document and a more reliable guide to events than the surviving Greek versions.[30] The *Revelatio* was widely disseminated in the Latin West, often circulating with a group of works, including the *Epistula Severi*, which described the circumstances of the discovery of Stephen's relics, their dispersal, and the miracles produced by them.[31] In 1946 critical editions of two Latin versions of the *Revelatio* were published by S. Vanderlinden, who distinguished a shorter version (Λ) from the longer and, in his opinion, more authoritative version (B).[32] The Latin versions A and B differ principally in the amount of detail they offer rather than in substantive matters. They complement one another and present a basically coherent account.

Lucian dates his initial vision quite precisely to Friday, 3 December 415 (A, 3). He explains that as he lay in his customary sleeping quarters in the baptistry, he was visited in a vision by a tall, elderly man with a long beard and handsome face, wearing gilded boots and a white mantle embroidered with gold crosses. He ordered Lucian to carry a message to Bishop John of Jerusalem, inquiring why John had left them shut up so long, for it was right that they be revealed during John's episcopate (B, 4–6). Under questioning, the elderly man identified himself as the Rabbi Gamaliel, who had instructed St Paul and who was afterwards made an apostle (B, 9).[33] He revealed further that he had been personally responsible for the burial of Stephen (cf. Acts 8: 2, 'certain devout men'), who had lain in the road outside Jerusalem as a feast for birds and wild

[30] The conclusion of P. Peeters, *Le Tréfonds oriental de l'hagiographie byzantine* (Brussels, 1950), 53–8.

[31] These works are collected in *PL* 41. 805–54.

[32] S. Vanderlinden, 'Revelatio Sancti Stephani', *REByz* 4 (1946), 178–217; 180 n. 18 for references to publication of the non-Latin versions. The Latin version B is roughly 50% longer than version A. I refer to the *Revelatio Sancti Stephani* with Vanderlinden's versions A and B with section numbers. The Greek and Latin recensions are discussed by J. Martin, 'Die Revelatio S. Stephani und Verwandtes', *HJ* 77 (1958), 419–33.

[33] Gamaliel's tolerant views toward the apostles are attested at Acts 5: 34–9.

animals. Since he knew Stephen's sanctity, faith, and devotion, and since he believed that he would have a part in the resurrection along with Stephen, Gamaliel had ordered some of the Christian faithful to carry Stephen's body to his own family estate (Kefar Gamala) north of the city, to mourn over him for forty days, and to bury him in the family crypt (B, 10–11). Gamaliel informed Lucian that on this property north of the city walls there lay buried together four bodies: Gamaliel himself, Stephen, Abibas, a son of Gamaliel who had died at the age of twenty, and, finally, Nicodemus, who is alleged here to have been Gamaliel's nephew. Nicodemus, like Stephen, had accepted Jesus and had been baptized by Peter and John. The baptism, however, enraged the High Priests, who ordered him beaten and cast outside the city. Gamaliel brought him back to his estate, nursed him unsuccessfully and, after his death, buried him in the family crypt at Stephen's feet (B, 12–13).

Wary of Satan's snares, Lucian failed to deliver the message to Bishop John. On the following Friday, Gamaliel returned, urging Lucian to obey his command and informing him how to distinguish the bodies in the crypt (B, 18–24). On the third Friday, Gamaliel returned again, exceedingly angry, and threatened Lucian into obedience (B, 25–33). On hearing Lucian's account of his dreams, John of Jerusalem's reaction was unhesitating and exuberant:

Blessed be the Lord God, the Son of the Living God. If, my beloved one, you saw these things and God revealed them to you just as you say, it is right that I transfer from that spot the blessed Stephen, the first martyr and the first deacon of Christ, who was the first to wage the Lord's wars (*dominica bella*) against the Jews and who, although he was placed on earth, saw God standing in heaven and who appeared like an angel in a public meeting of men.    (B, 34)

The failure of an initial search, however, prompted another nocturnal intervention by Gamaliel, who appeared this time to a monk called Migetius and provided him with instructions which led the search party to the appropriate spot. John himself, accompanied by the Bishops Eutonius of Sebaste and Eleutherius of Jericho, led the digging party. When they discovered a stone inscribed in Greek letters with the words

'Celiel, Nasoam, Gamaliel, Abibas', they knew they had found the right spot. John himself, claims Lucian, interpreted the Hebrew inscription (*hebraïca verba*, Aramaic?), identifying Celiel as Stephen, Nasoam as Nicodemus and Abibas as the son of Gamaliel (A, 43; B, 43). As they triumphantly disinterred the remains of St Stephen the Protomartyr, the earth shook and a fragrance issued from the crypt such as none of them had ever experienced and which made them think of the sweetness of paradise. Moreover, the healing powers which would become so conspicuous a part of Stephen's cult manifested themselves immediately. Seventy-three people were relieved of a host of maladies within the hour of the discovery of the relics (B, 46–7).

The importance of the Jewish environment is signalled in the *Revelatio* by the inscription with the Hebrew names 'Celiel, Nasoam, Gamaliel, Abibas' in Greek letters. Lucian informs us that he himself heard Bishop John interpret the inscription.[34] John knew the local languages, which was appropriate since Christians were a minority in Palestine and relations between Christians and Jews a constant problem.[35] More striking, however, is John's identification of Stephen as the 'first to wage the Lord's wars (*dominica bella*) against the Jews' (B, 34), an allusion which must be seen against a background of close proximity and constant competition between the two religions, as well as increasing tensions between the two groups in the early years of the fifth century. Only two months previously, on 20 October 415, Gamaliel VI, Patriarch of Jerusalem, had suffered a serious blow when the Emperors Honorius and Theodosius deprived him of his Praetorian Prefecture, an honorary title that accorded the Jewish Patriarch a rank equal to the highest imperial officials. Furthermore, Gamaliel was ordered to cease building synagogues, adjudicating legal disputes, and countenancing the circumcision of non-Jews.[36] But John, like many

[34] *Revelatio* A, 43: *Invenimus igitur altissimis litteris scriptum lapidem obrutum habentem ita: Celihel, quod interpretatur Stephanus Dei, et Nasoam, quod interpretatur Nicodemus, et Gamaliel. (Hoc interpretatus est papa Ioannes, sicut et ipse audivi ab ipso sancto episcopo)*; B, 43: *invenimus lapidem in quo sculptum erat: Celiel, Nasoam, Gamaliel, Abibas, hebraïca quidem verba, litteris autem graecis. Interpretatio vero nominum haec est: Celiel Stephanus dicitur, Nasoam vero Nicodemus, Abibas filium Gamalielis significat.*

[35] van Esbroeck, 'Jean II de Jérusalem' 109 notes John's attention to Jewish ritual in his speech for the dedication of the Church of Saint Sion in 394. The dedication ceremonies coincided with Yom Kippur.

[36] *CTh* 16. 8. 22 (415).

other bishops, may have been less concerned with Jews outside the church than with Judaizing Christians inside the church. The problem for many bishops was precisely that the two groups, Jews and Christians, often refused to remain distinct, and John's outburst about Stephen's 'wars' against the Jews may betray indirect criticism of Judaizing tendencies among local Christians who lived in a heavily Jewish environment. Stephen's relics and the development of his cult may have been useful to John in his dealings both with local Jews and with Judaizing Christians in his own congregation.[37] In December 415, however, John's mind was focused not on Jews or Judaizers, but on the ecclesiastical struggle in which he was deeply embroiled.

The discovery of Stephen's relics came at an opportune moment for Bishop John, who in late 415 was mired in the dispute concerning the teachings of the British monk Pelagius, whose views on grace, free will, and original sin brought him into sharp conflict with Augustine and Catholic orthodoxy. The Pelagian controversy brought together a remarkable array of personalities in the Holy Land in 415.[38] Pelagius himself had arrived in Palestine in about 411 and had found favour with Bishop John. But he also found in Jerome an adversary as formidable as Augustine. In addition to John, Jerome, and Pelagius himself were two men who would play a crucial role in the dissemination of the relics of Stephen: Avitus and Orosius, both from Braga (Roman *Bracara Augusta*) in the north-western province of Spain known as Galicia (or *Gallaecia*, as the Romans said). Avitus was a priest who had been in earlier years a correspondent of Jerome and who had lived in the Holy Land since about 409.[39] He participated in the opposition to Pelagius, but he is best known for his role in the dissemination of Stephen's relics. When the relics were discovered in December 415, it was Avitus who urged Lucian to dictate an account of his dreams, their verification, and the subsequent unearth-

---

[37] C. Ginzburg, 'La conversione degli ebrei di Minorca (417–418)', *Quaderni storici*, 79 (1992), 283–4. On Jewish–Christian relations in the Holy Land, see G. Stemberger, *Juden und Christen im Heiligen Land: Palästina unter Konstantin und Theodosius* (Munich, 1987).

[38] On the Pelagian controversy, see G. Bonner, *St. Augustine of Hippo: Life and Controversies*[2] (Norwich, 1986), 312–51.

[39] On Avitus, see B. Altaner, 'Avitus von Braga', *ZKG* 60 (1941), 456–68.

ing of the relics. He also acquired some of the relics from Lucian with the intention of sending them home to Spain, which was in turmoil at the time due to warring barbarian tribes.[40] He himself quickly translated Lucian's Greek account into Latin, which he then dispatched along with some relics and a letter of explanation to Bishop Balconius of Braga.[41]

Orosius too was a Spanish priest, though a younger man born probably in the mid-380s in Braga, where apparently he lived and witnessed the effects of the invasion and occupation of the Iberian peninsula by German tribes in September 409.[42] In 413 or 414 he left Spain for North Africa to consult with Augustine about Origenism and Priscillianism, either because he was confused and needed clarification about certain issues, or because he wanted to enlist Augustine's support against the spread of Priscillianism in his homeland. In 415 he wrote a brief work for Augustine entitled *Commonitorium de errore Priscillianistarum et Origenistarum*, to which Augustine responded with a treatise *Ad Orosium contra Priscillianistas et Origenistas.*[43] Augustine, however, soon dispatched him to Palestine to learn more about the origin of the soul from Jerome and, perhaps, to assist Jerome in the struggle against Pelagius. Orosius arrived at Jerome's monastery in 415, duly provided with a letter in which Augustine recommended him as 'alert of mind, ready of speech, burning with eagerness'.[44]

Although Pelagius had departed for the Holy Land in about 411, opposition to him and his associates continued to build in North Africa. In 412 a synod in Carthage condemned the views of one of Pelagius' disciples, Caelestius, and excommunicated him when he refused to abjure them. Reports of the controversy in the West and the opposition of Jerome eventually persuaded the Eastern bishops that the matter had to be investigated. In July 415 Pelagius was summoned to appear

[40] Cf. *Ep. Aviti* 3: *per totas iam Hispanias hoste diffuso.*

[41] Editions of the *Epistula Aviti* in *PL* 41. 805–8 and Vanderlinden, 'Revelatio Sancti Stephani', 188–9.

[42] For the sources of the events and dates of Orosius' life, see B. Lacroix, *Orose et ses idées* (Montreal, 1965), 29–39; E. Corsini, *Introduzione alle 'Storie' de Orosio* (Turin, 1968), 9–33; P. Fabbrini, *Paolo Orosio, uno storico* (Rome, 1979), 48–69.

[43] Texts of the *Commonitorium* and the *Ad Orosium* in *CCL* 49.

[44] Aug. *Ep.* 166. 2: *Religiosus iuvenis, catholica pace frater, aetate filius, honore conpresbyter noster Orosius, vigil ingenio, promptus eloquio, flagrans studio.*

before a synod presided over by John of Jerusalem. Orosius too was summoned, since he was in a position to provide information on events concerning Pelagius and his followers in North Africa. The synod proved turbulent and unruly, however, for John was unsympathetic to the accusations against Pelagius, and Pelagius' accusers, particularly Orosius, refused to be intimidated or even respectful.[45] The accusers failed to secure condemnation at this synod, but they succeeded in convening another synod at Diospolis in December 415 under the primate of Palestine, Bishop Eulogius of Caesarea. Once again, however, Pelagius would be vindicated.[46]

According to the *Revelatio Sancti Stephani*, Lucian's night vision came to him on 3 December 415, but it was not until two weeks later, after his second and third visions, that he reported to John what he had seen. The news that the tomb had been located was brought to John on 20 December while he was sitting with his fellow bishops in judgment of Pelagius at Diospolis. John quickly proceeded to the spot and recovered the relics, accompanied by two other bishops, Eutonius of Sebaste and Eleutherius of Jericho. The discovery of Stephen's relics must have created a sensation. Stephen was no shadowy figure whose martyrdom was recounted in an obscure text of dubious authenticity. He was a genuine figure from apostolic times, the first of all the martyrs, and his story was recounted in one of the church's canonical books. Even John's most committed opponents would be forced to rejoice at the discovery and to stifle their criticism in his hour of triumph. Moreover, the relics had come to light a mere six days before Stephen's designated feast day, 26 December.[47] On that day, in an *adventus* ceremony which must have brought forth the entire Christian population of the city, John solemnly deposited Stephen's relics in the Church of St Sion, the episcopal seat of Jerusalem. The relics would remain in Saint Sion for nearly twenty years until, on 15 May 439, they would be transferred in

[45] The only account of this synod is found in Orosius' *Liber Apologeticus* 3–6. For a more detailed narrative than I give here, see Bonner, *St. Augustine of Hippo* 332–4.

[46] For a full account of the synod and the doctrinal issues at stake, see Bonner, *St. Augustine of Hippo*, 334–8.

[47] On Stephen's feast day, see the article 'Saint Etienne' in *Vie des saints et des bienheureux selon l'ordre du calendrier avec l'historique des fêtes*, xii (Décembre; (Paris, 1956), 687–702, esp. 698–700.

a lavish ceremony to the new Basilica of St Stephen constructed on the alleged site of his martyrdom.[48]

Stephen's relics began to travel almost immediately after their discovery, first to North Africa and Minorca, and some years later to Constantinople.[49] Only on Minorca, however, would Stephen be mobilized in a campaign against the Jews.[50] John had failed to gather up all of the numinous treasure, and the priest Lucian had quietly reserved some of Stephen's remains for himself. Avitus sent his Latin translation of Lucian's account and some relics of Stephen, and not just 'dust', but 'solid bones', via Orosius to Bishop Balconius of Braga.[51] Orosius, however, did not sail directly for Spain, since he had promised Augustine in the previous year that he would return to Spain via North Africa. He kept his word by returning to Africa in summer 416, carrying the relics of Stephen, Avitus' Latin translation of Lucian's narrative, the minutes of the

[48] On the site of Stephen's martyrdom and the basilicas constructed there, see M.-J. Lagrange, *Saint Étienne et son sanctuaire à Jérusalem* (Paris, 1894); P. Peeters, 'Le Sanctuaire de la lapidation de S. Étienne', *AnalBoll* 27 (1908), 359–68. The original basilica built for Stephen was dedicated in 439. The Empress Eudocia, who lived in Jerusalem during the years 438–9 and from 444 to her death in 460, particularly venerated Stephen and constructed in his honour a grander and more sumptuous basilica which was consecrated, still unfinished, in June 460. Its ruins were discovered in 1882 and later excavated, a summary of which can be found in H. Vincent and F.-M. Abel, *Jérusalem: Recherches de topographie, d'archéologie et d'histoire*, ii: *Jérusalem nouvelle* (Paris, 1926), fasc. 4. 766–804.

[49] The date of the dispersal of relics to Constantinople is unclear. The 9th-cent. chronicler Theophanes Confessor, *Chronographia*, a. m. 5920 (ed. de Boor, 1. 86–7) claims that Pulcheria, sister of the Emperor Theodosius II, received relics of Stephen in Constantinople in 427. It is troubling, however, that no contemporary source mentions so important an event. The account of Theophanes is accepted, but redated to 421, by K. G. Holum and G. Vikan, 'The Trier Ivory, *Adventus* Ceremonial, and the Relics of St. Stephen', *DOP* 33 (1979), 113–33; and K. Holum, 'Pulcheria's Crusade AD 421–22 and the Ideology of Imperial Victory', *GRBS* 18 (1977), 163 n. 46. It is certain that in 439 the Empress Eudocia carried relics of Stephen from Jerusalem to Constantinople and deposited them in the church built by Pulcheria in honour of St Lawrence. On Eudocia's involvement in Stephen's cult, see E. A. Clark, 'Claims on the Bones of Saint Stephen: The Partisans of Melania and Eudocia', *ChHist* 51 (1982), 141–56.

[50] On Stephen's cult in North Africa, see H. Delehaye, 'Les Premiers "libelli miraculorum"', *AnalBoll* 29 (1910), 427– 34; id., 'Les Receuils antiques des miracles des saints', *AnalBoll* 43 (1925), 74–85; C. Lambot, 'Les Sermons de Saint Augustin pour les fêtes des martyrs', *AnalBoll* 67 (1949), 249– 66; V. Saxer, *Morts, martyrs, reliques en Afrique chrétienne aux premiers siècles* (Paris, 1980); Y. Duval, *Loca Sanctorum Africae: Le Culte des martyrs en Afrique du IV^e au VII^e siècle*, 2 vols. (Rome, 1982).

[51] *Ep. Aviti* 8: *misi vobis per sanctum filium et compresbyterum meum Orosium reliquias de corpore beati Stephani primi martyris, hoc est pulverem carnis atque nervorum et, quod fidelius certiusque credendum est, ossa solida.*

Council of Diospolis, and a packet of letters from Jerome.[52] Orosius later sailed to Minorca with the intention of making the crossing to the Spanish mainland. Deterred, however, by the chaotic conditions caused by ongoing warfare, he decided to return again to Africa, but not before depositing some of Stephen's relics at a church outside Magona, the town on the eastern end of the island.[53]

But when exactly did Stephen's relics arrive on the island? The date of their arrival hinges on the travels and literary activity of Orosius in the years 416–17. When Orosius returned to North Africa in June–July 416, Augustine was completing Books 6–10 of the *City of God*, his great refutation of the charge that abandonment of the old gods had caused the empire's present calamities. Part of his response was to argue that pagans, in their obsession with present evils, conveniently ignored or forgot the countless calamities that had befallen the empire prior to the triumph of Christianity and the prohibition of sacrifices. But he found the task of chronicling historical disasters distasteful.[54] His solution was to enlist Orosius for that task. Between June–July 416, the date of his return from the Holy Land, and the end of 417, the end date of the narrative, Orosius laboured to fulfil Augustine's request. The result of his efforts was the work for which he is best known, the *History against the Pagans*, a universal history of the world from Adam to his own day with polemical emphasis on the calamities that had befallen the Romans and preceding empires before the coming of Christ.[55]

Orosius' biographers have invariably assumed that he com-

[52] Aug. *Ep*. 166. 2 to Jerome discusses Orosius' character and the pledge to return to Africa before proceeding to Spain. Aug. *Ep*. 172 is Jerome's reply to Augustine. Aug. *Ep*. 175. 1 mentions Orosius' arrival in Carthage in June–July 416.

[53] *Ep. Sev*. 4. 2.

[54] Cf. *De Civ. Dei* 2. 17 (*CSEL* 40(1). 82): *multa commemorare iam piget foeda et iniusta*; 3. 17 (p. 136): *quid itaque ego tantas moras vel scribens patiar, vel lecturis adferam?*): 3. 18 (p. 141): *si enarrare vel commemorare conemur, nihil aliud quam scriptores etiam nos erimus historiae*; 3. 21 (p. 147): *multa enim praetereo*; 3. 31 (p. 159): *ut omittam cetera . . . et alia multo plura quae commemorare longum putavi*. At 4. 2 (p. 164), he expresses regret that he has said nothing of all the natural disasters that afflicted the empire without the intervention of the gods, but laments the enormity of the task, *Si haec adque huius modi, quae habet historia, unde possem, colligere voluissem, quando finissem* ('If I had wished to collect from history wherever I could, these and similar instances, when would I have finished?').

[55] On his task as he conceived it, see Oros. *Hist. praef.*

posed the *History* in 416–17 and then sailed to Minorca in autumn or winter 417, but two pieces of evidence, previously overlooked, suggest that this assumption is incorrect. Augustine extracted the promise, when he recommended Orosius to Jerome in 415, that Orosius would return to North Africa in the following year *on his way back to Spain*.[56] Severus' assertion that he was coming from Jerusalem when he stayed briefly on Minorca (4. 1: *ab Hierosolyma veniens, Magonae non longo tempore immoratus est*) confirms that the stopover in North Africa had been merely that and nothing more. He apparently left Africa almost immediately after discharging his obligation to Augustine, and learned on Minorca, in late summer or autumn 416, that fighting had broken out again on the mainland and that the overland trip to Galicia would be too hazardous. He then returned to North Africa, perhaps to wait out the war, perhaps to take up permanent residence. At this point, when Orosius was a refugee with no other commitments, Augustine made his request, which Orosius laboured to fulfil for the next year and a half, finishing the *History against the Pagans* in late 417 or early 418.[57] This revised chronology reveals that the impression conveyed by Severus at 4. 3–4 of an outbreak of religious fervour leading to a rapid, miraculous conversion is fundamentally misleading. The relics destined for Bishop Balconius of Braga arrived on Minorca in late summer or autumn 416, not 417. Severus' campaign against the Jews had thus been in progress for over a year before the final march on Magona in February 418.

V. JEWS AND CHRISTIANS ON MINORCA

Little is known about Christianity in the Balearic Islands before the events recounted in the *Epistula Severi*. Saint Paul had intended to travel to Spain (cf. Rom. 15: 28), and Theodoret of Cyrrhus in the fifth century preserves a tradition that Paul

---

[56] Aug. *Ep*. 166. 2: *rogavi eum ut abs te veniens per nos ad propria remearet*.

[57] A number of theories, all of them unconvincing, have been offered to solve the time compression at this point in Orosius' career. See Lacroix, *Orose et ses idées*, 40–5; Corsini, *Introduzione alle 'Storie' de Orosio*, 27–33; Fabbrini, *Paolo Orosio*, 57–62. The most persuasive treatment of the chronological problems is that of Corsini.

actually did set out for Spain, but his testimony is supported by no other source.[58] Only in the fourth century do we begin to get evidence of Christians on these islands, although the Christian communities were probably much older. A few humble inscriptions, the odd ring with the Christian symbol of a fish and anchor, some fourth- and fifth-century ceramic engraved with the sign of the cross—exiguous remains of this sort are all that attest to fourth-century Christianity in the Balearics.[59] In fact, barely a dozen Christian inscriptions survive from the Balearics in the whole period before the Arab invasions, and all but one of these are from Majorca.[60] Although poor in inscriptions, Minorca is rich in early Christian basilicas, of which four have been discovered, at Puerto de Fornells on the north-east coast, Iletta del Rey in Port Mahón, Es Fornás de Torelló near Mahón, and San Bou on the coast 10 km. to the south of Alayor. These basilicas all appear to have been fifth- or early sixth-century foundations and certainly attest to a strong Christian presence on the island in the fifth century.[61] The basilica at San Bou has attracted particular attention, since it is the oldest and best preserved of the four, and its remains are compatible with a date of construction even earlier than the mid-fifth century, possibly as early as the late fourth.[62] G. Seguí and J. Hillgarth even wished to believe that the basilica at San Bou was the 'new basilica' (cf. 30. 2) which the Jews of Magona built on the site of their burned-out synagogue.[63] None the less, our knowledge of the social and religious life of Minorca's

[58] Theodoret of Cyrrhus, *Interp. of 2 Tim.* (*PG* 82. 856).

[59] C. Veny, 'Early Christianity in the Balearic Islands', *Classical Folia*, 21 (1967), 210–23. Apart from the *Ep. Sev.*, the earliest document mentioning bishops on the Balearics is the *Notitia Provinciarum et Civitatum Africae*, containing a list of bishops who attended a Council of Carthage in 484. Under *insulae Sardiniae* are listed three Balearic bishops: *Macarius de Minorica*, *Helias de Maiorica*, and *Opilio de Ebuso* (*CSEL* 7. 133–4). Severus is the first attested Minorcan bishop.

[60] C. Veny, *Corpus de las inscripciones balearicas hasta la dominacion arabe* (Rome, 1965).

[61] On Minorca's basilicas and their dates, see P. de Palol, *Arqueologia cristiana de la España romana. Siglos IV–VI* (Madrid, 1967), 15–28.

[62] De Palol, *Arqueologia cristiana* 16–8, 27.

[63] G. Seguí Vidal and J. N. Hillgarth, *La 'Altercatio' y la basilica paleocristiana de Son Bou de Menorca* (Palma de Majorca, 1955), 28–31. Seguí and Hillgarth suggested that the pseudo-Augustinian *Altercatio Ecclesiae contra Synagogam* might be Severus' *commonitorium* (8. 1) and that the *altercatio* took place at Son Bou. These hypotheses were rightly dismissed by de Palol, *Arqueologia cristiana*, 16 n. 32: 'suposiciones que no tienen fundamento alguno'.

Christians in the early fifth century must be culled almost exclusively from the *Epistula Severi* itself.

The settlement of Jews in the far west of the Mediterranean was the result primarily of the massive defeats of the insurrections in Palestine in 66–70 and 132–5, the first of which resulted in the enslavement and deportation to the west of large numbers of Jews, while the second defeat led to an even greater diaspora. Jewish communities in Spain first appear in our sources in the third century, and their presence is well attested in many places in the fourth century, particularly in the east and south of the country.[64] The fact that nothing is said about them in the Balearics is hardly surprising, in light of the poor documentation concerning the islands, but we can assume that Jews settled in the Balearics quite early. Both Majorca and Minorca have good harbours and were routine stopping places for sea traffic plying its way between the coasts of Italy, Gaul, Spain, and North Africa. The Balearics were thus well placed on the migration route westward. But, as in the case of Christians, we must turn to Severus himself to learn about the social and religious life of Minorca's Jews.

Severus addresses his letter to the Christians of the entire world, among whom he is particularly interested in his fellow bishops, as the frequent allusions to 'your Blessedness' suggest (1. 2; 8. 2; 9. 4; 31. 1). So broad a reading public will not, however, be acquainted with Minorca, so Severus opens his letter with a description of the geographical setting. He explains that Minorca is one of the Balearic Islands, located almost midway between Mauretania and Spain. The island is small, roughly thirty miles long and ten miles wide at its widest point (2. 3), and has a dry, rugged landscape. As Severus himself is the 'most unworthy of all men' (*pref.*; 2. 6; 8. 2; 9. 3), so Minorca is the 'most forsaken of all lands' (2. 5), the 'ends of the earth' (31. 4), and 'this little world' (20. 21), conspicuous for its 'tiny size, dryness, and harshness' (2. 5). God's exaltation of the 'lowly of this world' [1 Cor. 1: 28] applies not only to people, but to places as well (2. 4).

---

[64] The evidence for Jews in Roman Spain (1st–4th cent.) is compiled by W. P. Bowers, 'Jewish Communities in Spain in the Time of Paul the Apostle', *JThS* NS 26 (1975), 395–402; see also L. Garcia Iglesias, *Los judios en la España antigua* (Madrid, 1978).

The island's two 'small towns', Jamona (modern Ciudadela)
and Magona (modern Mahón), have distinct religious charac-
ters. 'Even now,' claims Severus, Jamona, the bishop's seat,
enjoys an 'ancient favour' from God, since Jews are 'absolutely
unable to live there' (3. 1). Tradition maintained that Jews in
Jamona would fall sick or drop dead or even be 'struck down
by a thunderbolt'. They no longer even tried, claims Severus, to
settle in Jamona (3. 2). On the other hand, there was in the rival
town of Magona on the eastern end of the island a thriving
Jewish community. Severus is consistent in his claim that all
Minorca's Jews, who numbered approximately 540 (cf. 29. 2),
lived in Magona. Moreover, the Jewish gentry clearly
dominated the town socially and perhaps religiously. As
Severus puts it, Magona 'seethed with so great a multitude of
Jews, as if with vipers and scorpions, that Christ's church was
being wounded by them daily' (3. 6). Magona's Christians are
'humble in heart as well as physical strength, yet superior by
the force of truth' (6. 4), and the conversion of the Jews is
characterized as a 'victory which no one dared hope for and
which no one could expect' (8. 3). Christian weakness, particularly in Magona, is indeed a prominent and recurring
theme in the letter.

But how reliable is this picture of Minorca? Should we infer
that these 'small towns' were really little more than villages and
that Magona's Christians were a tiny minority in an essentially
Jewish town? I suspect that this picture is misleading on two
counts.[65] Livy (28. 37. 9) reports that during the Second Punic
War, in 206/5 BC, the Carthaginians were able to recruit 2,000
slingers from Minorca alone, and Diodorus Siculus (5. 17. 2),
writing in the first century BC, claims that Majorca and
Minorca together had a population of more than 30,000. Moreover, Magona had been made a *municipium* in the early empire
(cf. *CIL* 2. 3708), which is hardly surprising since it possesses
one of the best harbours in the entire Mediterranean. These
towns undoubtedly were small, but we should be wary of
demoting them to the status of villages. From the disparate
pieces of evidence available, I would infer that Magona and

[65] Cf. R. Van Dam, *Leadership and Community in Late Antique Gaul* (Berkeley, 1985),
67: 'Previously Jews and Christians had divided the island, each community segregated
into its own small village and each with its own religious leader.'

Jamona had populations of between one and three thousand people each in 418. Concerning the number of Christians in Magona, it is worth noting that the repeated emphasis on Christian weakness has a rhetorical purpose, for it helps to deflect responsibility for this blatantly illegal affair away from the Christian majority and on to Christ himself, who 'achieved everything with his own forces and without us even uttering a word' (8. 3). The evidence of the letter, however, strongly suggests that the weakness of the local Christians was due to the social and political prestige of the Jewish gentry, not to numerical inferiority. The Christians had after all been waging a campaign against Magona's Jews for over a year before the confrontation in February 418. This campaign proved ineffective because of the prominence of the Jewish notables and because the Jewish community, recalling the martyrdom of the Maccabees, vowed to fight to the death in defence of their religion (8. 4).

Severus' claim of religious rivalry between Magona and Jamona is convincing, since competition between towns was normal, but he passes over in silence an obvious third party, the pagans. Inscriptions from an earlier period attest the worship on Minorca of Juno and the Great Mother, but Severus' letter gives the impression that pagans have disappeared by his day.[66] That impression is surely misleading, for pagans are well attested on the mainland in the Visigothic period and we should assume that they were still part of Minorca's religious scene.[67] But they play no role in the events of February 418. Severus is also silent on the issue of economic and political rivalry between the two towns. In preventing Jews from settling in Jamona, God appears to have done them a favour, since Magona was probably in antiquity, as in modern times, the more vibrant town with its superb harbour. Moreover, all the evidence in the letter concerning municipal offices concerns Magona, and it is possible that Magona's magistrates and council had jurisdiction over the entire island. We find some support for this hypothesis in an early imperial inscription

---

[66] Veny, *Corpus de las inscripciones balearicas*, no. 176 (Juno), no. 119 (Great Mother).

[67] On the continued presence of the *pagani*, see, most recently, J. N. Hillgarth, 'Popular Religion in Visigothic Spain', in E. James, *Visigothic Spain: New Approaches* (Oxford, 1980), 11–18.

found at Mahón, in which a Maecius Maecianus contrasts his service as *duumvir* 'on the island' with his flaminate on the mainland in Hispania Tarraconensis (*CIL* 2. 3711: *ter duumviratu in insula functus etiam flaminatu provinciae Hispaniae citerioris*). If this suggestion is correct, then Severus' resentment against the Jewish gentry of Magona has all the more point, since they dominate not only Magona but the whole island.

The *Epistula* is frustratingly uninformative about individual Christians. We learn that Severus had become bishop at 'about the same period' that Orosius visited the island (4. 1), that is, in late summer or autumn 416.[68] Thus, he was a relatively new bishop, having been in office for about a year and a half. He tells us nothing of his background, but his simple and unsophisticated literary style reveals the absence of a Classical education.[69] Although the family name is attested on Minorcan inscriptions from the early empire, there is no way to connect these with our Severus.[70] There is mention of only one member of the Christian gentry, Julius, a *vir honoratus*, which implies that he served in the imperial civil service (20. 5). There is also an allusion to the presence of monks on Minorca at this time (10. 1; 20. 4).[71]

By way of contrast with the paucity of evidence about Christians, the *Epistula Severi* offers a wealth of information about the Jews of Magona. At the head of the synagogue stands Theodorus, whom Severus calls a 'teacher of the Law (*doctor legis*) and, if I may use their own phrase, the Father of Fathers' (6. 2). Theodorus' titles raise a number of interesting questions. First, he was apparently not referred to as a rabbi, at least not in

---

[68] On the date of Orosius' visit, see above pp. 24–5.

[69] On his style, note the observation of C. Paucker, 'De latinitate scriptorum quorundam saeculi quarti et ineuntis quinti p. C. minorum observationes', *Zeitschrift fur die österreichischen Gymnasien*, 32 (1881), 482: 'Delectabilior legenti est Severi episcopi Maioricensis [*sic*] epistula . . . inartificiali ac prope rusticiore sermone conscripta (*c.*418, ut putant).'

[70] Veny, *Corpus de las inscripciones balearicas*, from Mahón: no. 128 (dedication of Julia Severa and her husband to their son who had been aedile and duovir), no. 129 (dedication of Julia Severa to her husband, Quintus Caecilius Philistio), no. 130 (dedication of Quintus Caecilius Philistio to Caecilia Severa, *patrona optima*).

[71] Demougeot, 'L'Évêque Sévère', 23 adduces Augustine, *Ep.* 48 (AD 398), addressed to Eudoxius, abbot of a monastery on Capraria, as evidence of monks in the Balearics from the end of the 4th cent. But Eudoxius was abbot of a monastery on the Capraria north-east of Corsica, not the little island of Capraria south of Majorca (cf. *RE* 3. 1546). Hence, the monks in the *Ep. Sev.* cannot be from Capraria.

the formal sense. He was not a Talmudic scholar educated and 'ordained' in the schools of Palestine by those rabbis who shaped the course of Rabbinical Judaism. The term 'rabbi', which would later become conventional, is attested in only a handful of instances in late Roman inscriptions in the western empire, usually in the form *rebbi* (gen. *rebbitis*, nom. pl. *rebbites*).[72] On the other hand, Theodorus certainly was a 'rabbi' in its informal sense of 'teacher' (cf. John 1: 38; 20: 16), even if the term was not used in his community. There was, in fact, no uniform title in the diaspora for the learned exegetes who taught and expounded Jewish Law, but the variety of titles referring to teachers and students of the Law attests that study of the Law was a central activity for diaspora Jews. In Roman inscriptions alone, we find a *didaskalos* (*CIJ* i². 333), a *mathetes* (*CIJ* i². 190), a *mathetes sophon* (*CIJ* i². 508), three instances of *nomomathes* (*CIJ* i². 113, 193, 333), and a *nomodidaskalos* (*CIJ* i². 201), the last of which is especially interesting since it is an exact Greek equivalent of *doctor legis*.[73] Theodorus thus has a 'rabbinical' role as teacher and exegete of the Law. He is relied upon by the whole community for his 'knowledge' (6. 1) and because he is recognized as 'more learned than the others' (19. 9), but he was not the only teacher of the Law on Minorca. When Jewish resistance finally crumbled, a number of those who accompanied Theodorus to the church were thought of by Severus as *doctores legis*: 'aged teachers of the Law (*inveterati illi legis doctores*) began to believe, without any verbal wrangling, without any dispute over the Scriptures' (21. 5). Another Jewish notable, Innocentius, is referred to as learned in Classical literature, both Greek and Latin, and as 'meditating constantly on the Law' (18. 15). Taken together, these passages suggest that a number of the prominent members of Magona's

[72] S. J. D. Cohen, 'Epigraphical Rabbis', *JQR* 72 (1981), 1– 17; Millar, 'The Jews of the Graeco-Roman Diaspora', 110–12.

[73] On the Roman inscriptions, see H. J. Leon, *The Jews of Ancient Rome* (Philadelphia, 1960), 167–94; cf. Acts 5: 34 (Gamaliel as *nomodidaskalos*). *Doctor legis* appears to be a non-technical term to describe men at any period of history who were learned in the Law. Jerome, for example, uses the word both of ancient interpreters of the Law (*Comm. on Jeremiah* 1. 19 [*CSEL* 59. 20]) and of the learned Jew who helped him with the proper names in Chronicles, many of which had become badly corrupted during the process of translation into Greek and Latin (*Pref. to Chronicles* [*PL* 29. 423]); cf. Tertullian, *Against Marcion* 4. 25 (*CSEL* 47. 507).

synagogue were learned in the Law and skilled in its exposition.[74]

Theodorus' formal title in the synagogue is Father of
Fathers, preserved in Greek (*pater pateron*, not *pater patrum*, as in
the *Patrologia*). It is attested (in Greek) in one other instance in a
funeral inscription for a Marcellus from the south Italian town
of Venusia (Venosa): ὧδε κεῖτε Μάρκελλος πατὴρ πατέρων καὶ
πάτρων τῆς πόλεως.[75] But the Latinized *pater patrum* also
occurs.[76] The fact that Severus preserves the title in Greek
suggests that the Jews of Magona still used Greek as their liturgical language in the synagogue. That would not be unusual.
Inscriptional evidence reveals that Greek was normally the
language of Western diaspora Jews in the early empire, and its
use in religious worship continued long after western Jews had
adopted Latin as their everyday language.[77] Minorca's Jews,
for example, clearly spoke Latin and were linguistically well
integrated into the surrounding culture. In one incident, Christians and Jews were marching through the streets on the way to
the synagogue when the Christians began to sing one of the
psalms. The Jews were able to pick up the tune and join in,
doubtless to turn the meaning of the verse back on their Christian opponents, 'Their memory has perished with a crash and
the Lord endures forever' [Ps. 9: 7–8] (13. 2).

Expertise in the Law was hardly the sole criterion in the
selection of a head of a synagogue, whether a *pater pateron*, as
here on Minorca, or, more usually, the *archisynagogos* or *princeps
synagogae*. Social prestige and the ability to lay out large sums of
money in benefaction to the community were also greatly
sought after.[78] The Jews particularly rely on Theodorus for his

[74] See S. Safrai, 'Education and the Study of the Torah', in *CRINT* 2. 945–70, esp.
958–69 on adult study-groups.

[75] *JIWE* i 114 (= *CIJ* i² 619b).

[76] *JIWE* i 85 (= *CIJ* i² 607), 68 (= *CIJ* i² 610), 90 (= *CIJ* i² 614), in all of which the
phrase occurs in the abbreviated form PP, originally restored as *p(rae)p(ositus)*, but now
read as *p(ater) p(atrum)*. See Noy's commentary on *JIWE* i 68.

[77] See V. Colorni, 'L'uso del greco nella liturgia del guidaismo ellenistico e la novella
146 di Giustiniano', *Annali di storia del diritto*, 8 (1964), 19–80.

[78] For a concise discussion of the role of the *archisynagogos*, see E. Schürer, *The History
of the Jewish People in the Age of Jesus Christ (175 BC–AD 135)*, ii (Edinburgh, 1979), 434–6.
The few attested instances of women and children as *archisynagogoi* illustrate well the
importance of wealth and social prestige, see Brooten, *Women Leaders*, 5–33; also, the

'influence' and because he is 'pre-eminent in both wealth and worldly honour not only among the Jews, but also among Magona's Christians' (6. 1). His younger brother refers to him as the 'pillar of our synagogue, in whom we placed all our trust' (18. 18; cf. 7. 1). Theodorus' influence thus extends far beyond the synagogue. As head of the synagogue, he would have enjoyed legal immunity from all obligations to the city council (*CTh* 16. 8. 2 [330]), but Severus informs us that he had fulfilled all those duties. In addition he had served in the past as *defensor civitatis*, a position created in the reign of Valentinian I (364–75) to provide expeditious and inexpensive adjudication of legal matters. The *defensor*'s primary task was to protect the weak from ruinously expensive and protracted litigation against the 'outrages of the powerful'.[79] In 409, Honorius and Theodosius decreed (*CJ* 1. 55. 8) that *defensores* should be men 'imbued with the sacred mysteries of orthodox religion' (*sacris orthodoxae religionis imbuti mysteriis*). They were to be appointed by the praetorian prefect after nomination by a council composed of the local bishop and clergy, the principal landowners, and the decurions. Augustine's *Ep*. 22*, written in March 420, confirms in vivid fashion the necessity of such officials in North Africa, and undoubtedly on Minorca as well. He complains of the helplessness of the clergy when faced with the high-handed conduct of *potentiores improbi*, and he wants Hippo to have a *defensor*. He is concerned that the man possess not only the appropriate moral qualities, but that he have a suitable rank (*dignitas*) so that he can successfully face down the powerful. Preferably, the man should be an imperial functionary (Valentinian's original intent), but if he has to be a *privatus* of curial status, then let him be given a rank that would grant him sufficient authority (*auctoritas*) to perform his job successfully.[80] Augustine's concern about the clout necessary to be a successful *defensor* should tell us something about Theodorus' position on Minorca. It is unclear when Theodorus had served as

---

recent discussion in G. H. R. Horsley, *New Documents Illustrating Early Christianity: A Review of the Greek Inscriptions and Papyri published in 1979* (Marrickville, N. S. W., 1987), 213–20.

[79] *CTh* 1. 29. 1, 3 (368?).

[80] Cf. F. Jacques, 'Le Défenseur de cité d'après la Lettre 22* de saint Augustin', *REAug* 32 (1986), 56–73.

*defensor*, but in the winter of 417/18, the *defensor* was Caecilianus, who ranked second in the synagogue after Theodorus
(19. 8). He, and probably Theodorus before him, had been
nominated by the local council, the principal landowners, and
the local bishop. These Jewish notables were hardly 'imbued
with the mysteries of sacred religion'. We have here a good
example of local populations quietly ignoring the distant
thunder of imperial edicts and arranging their affairs in accord-
ance with the reality of local power structures.

The title of *patronus* (6. 3) sums up perfectly Theodorus' social
and political dominance in Magona and perhaps on all of
Minorca. Other Jews are known to have been *patroni civitatis*, like
the Marcellus from Venosa, who offers an exact parallel to Theodorus, since he was likewise a Father of Fathers and Patron of the
City.[81] Theodorus' task as the *patronus* was, among other things,
to represent the local community in all its dealings—business,
legal, political—with the authorities in neighbouring Jamona
and in the greater world beyond Minorca's shores. He was
undoubtedly the wealthiest landowner in Magona and had, as
we shall presently see, social and family connections that
reached all the way to the imperial court.

Most of the Jewish notables mentioned in the *Epistula Severi*
are related to Theodorus in some way. Meletius, his younger
brother, figures prominently in the narrative. In the street riot
when Theodorus loses control of his community, Meletius flees
to the hills in the company of Innocentius, another high-born
Jew and a recent refugee from the warfare on the mainland.
Severus devotes a good portion of his narrative to the tale of
their ill-fated plan to flee the island (18). Meletius is married to
an Artemisia, whose conversion history is also presented in
abundant detail. She is the daughter of Litorius, who 'recently
governed this province and who is now said to be a Count' (24.
2). A Litorius is well known from events in Gaul in the 430s, but
he has not been adequately studied in connection with
Minorca because he has long, and erroneously, been known as
*Lectorius*, printed first by Baronius and later by Migne.
Meletius' father-in-law had recently (*nuper*) been governor of

---

[81] *JIWE* i 114 (= *CIJ* i² 619b): ὧδε κεῖτε Μάρκελλος πατὴρ πατέρων καὶ πάτρων τῆς
πόλεως; 115 (= *CIJ* i² 619c) (also from Venosa): ὧδε κεῖτε Αὐξάνειος πατὴρ καὶ πάτρων
τῆς πόλεως.

34

the Balearics, which had been administered in early imperial times as part of Hispania Tarraconensis. Between 369 and 389, they were made an independent province to be administered by a *praeses*. According to Severus, Litorius 'is now said to be a Count' (*comes esse dicitur*), which seems to imply that Severus has heard of Litorius' political promotion, but he does not know the man as he knows Theodorus and the local Minorcan Jews. Only one Litorius is attested in *The Prosopography of the Later Roman Empire*, and he played a prominent role in the defence of Gaul.[82] Litorius is confirmed as *comes rei militaris* in Gaul between 435 and 437, when he led Hunnish cavalry successfully against the Armoricans. In 439 he was second in command to Flavius Aetius, the most famous Roman general of the day, and had been promoted to the position of *magister utriusque militiae*. In his ambition to surpass the successes of Aetius, however, he rashly led his troops against the Visigoths near Toulouse in 439, having put his trust in pagan diviners and oracles.[83] His forces were annihilated, he himself was wounded and captured, and he later died in prison.

Some interesting conclusions follow from the fact that our Artemisia was the daughter of the well-known Count Litorius. In the first place, she was probably quite young, despite the impression created by Severus. He portrays her as a proud and strong-willed *femina nobilissima* (24. 1). She is a *matrona* (24. 4) and the mention of a nurse implies that she has a baby with her when she flees to the hills (24. 2). If she was, for example, 20 years old in 418, then her father Litorius must have been at least 40 to 45. He would then have been between age 61 and 66 when he was defeated in 439. That chronology is certainly possible, but it reveals that Artemisia is younger than we might have guessed.[84] Her imperiousness may have derived not from

---

[82] Testimonia in *PLRE* ii, s.v. Litorius.

[83] Prosper of Aquitaine, *Chronicon*, s.a. 439 (*MGH AA*, 9. 1, p. 476): *Litorius, qui secunda ab Aetio patricio potestate Chunis auxiliaribus praeerat, dum Aetii gloriam superare appetit dumque haruspicum responsis et daemonum significationibus fidit, pugnam cum Gothis inprudenter conseruit fecitque intelligi, quantum illa, quae cum eodem periit, manus prodesse potuerit, si potioris consiliis quam sua temeritate uti maluisset, quando tantam ipse hostibus cladem intulit, ut, nisi inconsideranter proelians captivitatem incidisset, dubitandum foret, cui potius parti victoria adscriberetur.*

[84] Inscriptional evidence from both the Eastern and Western empire offers examples of Jewish girls married by their mid-teens, sometimes as young as 12. See the useful

INTRODUCTION

maturity in years, but from superiority in social rank to those surrounding her, especially to the Catholic Bishop.

Even more interesting is the issue of Litorius' religious affiliation. Was he (1) a Jew, (2) a Christian, or (3) a pagan? In favour of his Judaism, we may cite his daughter's spirited resistance to forced conversion; in favour of his Christianity, the law of 418 (*CTh* 16. 8. 24) that excluded all Jews from the higher ranks of the civil and military administration; in favour of his paganism, the report of the chronicler Prosper of Aquitaine that he foolishly trusted in soothsayers and pagan diviners before his final defeat. We have here a good example of the difficulty of determining religious conviction with the kinds of evidence that survive from antiquity. The least likely possibility is that he was a pagan, the choice of *PLRE* ii (whose editors could not know that he was the father of our Artemisia). We should accept it as plausible that a Jew or a Christian, at a critical moment before a great battle, might avail himself of pagan divinatory 'technology', which was more highly developed than anything offered by Judaism or Christianity. It is more difficult to decide between the Jewish and Christian options. Jews were banned from high office, but, as we have observed, the requirement that *defensores* be orthodox Christians went unfulfilled on Minorca (and doubtless elsewhere), and it is equally doubtful that the ban on Jews in high office was consistently observed.[85] On the other hand, if Litorius was conspicuous in his adherence to Jewish customs, we might expect to hear of it from hostile Christians like Prosper after his defeat and disgrace in 439. The evidence offers no firm conclusion. If he succeeded in retaining his Jewish identity, then he offers an example of a well-born Jew holding high rank long after Jews were legally barred from such offices.[86] If, on the other hand,

collection of evidence in Horsley, *New Documents*, 221–9; also, S. M. Treggiari, *Roman Marriage* (Oxford, 1991), 398–403.

[85] For the ban on Jews in civil or military offices, see *CTh* 16. 8. 16 (404); *CTh* 16. 8. 24 (418); *Sirm. Const.* 6 *ad fin.* (425); *Nov. Theod.* 3. 2 (438); cf. Ps.-Aug. *De Alter. Eccl. et Syn. Dial.* (*PL* 42. 1133): (Ecclesia addressing Synagoga) *Iudaeum esse comitem non licet; senatum tibi introire prohibetur; praefecturam nescis; ad militiam non admitteris*.

[86] *CIJ* i² 103* from northern Italy in the 5th cent. offers a possible parallel: *Cham v(ir) c(larissimus) com(es) vir mir(a)e bonitatis.* Frey argued *ad loc.* that Cham cannot be a Jew because the name was execrated by Jews and the political status impossible, but the assumption that *CTh* 16. 8. 24 (418) was routinely enforced is probably incorrect.

Litorius had made his peace with the bishops and, like his daughter, had converted to Christianity, we may hypothesize an even more interesting religious life: public observance of Christian rites, private retention of many Jewish customs, and, at a moment of crisis, consultation of pagan soothsayers and diviners.

One other kinsman of Theodorus is mentioned in the *Epistula Severi*, and he is troubling for the historian since he is one of two Jews mentioned in the letter whose names appear to be fabrications. Are we really to believe that Theodorus has a young cousin named Galilaeus? Jews almost never named their children after geographical regions, least of all the region that had for generations been a byword for 'Christian'.[87] The name appears to be devised for the occasion, as does the name of another Jew called Reuben. In both instances, Severus draws attention to the special nature of the name. He, like many other early Christians, believes that God arranges human affairs so that the 'mystery of events' will be played out under 'appropriate names' (19. 3). He signals this theme twice in the letter, at the introductions of Reuben and later Galilaeus. Of Reuben, Severus writes:

a certain Jew called Reuben was chosen by the Lord (that appropriate names be preserved in all matters) to be made the first-born of them all. For he delighted the hearts of all with a most holy cry, praying that he be released from the chains of Jewish superstition. And without delay he became the 'first-born of Jacob' [Gen. 35: 23] and received the sign of salvation. (15. 1–3)

The name Reuben could be genuine, but it seems that Severus has devised it to dramatize his status as the 'first-born'. In a similar way, Severus notes the special significance of Galilaeus' name: 'in their first public meeting, a certain youth, a cousin of Theodorus himself, by the name of Galilaeus (that the mystery of events, as has often been said already, may be revealed to the end with appropriate names) began to proclaim . . .' (19. 3). After delivering an impassioned speech revealing his fear of Christian violence, Galilaeus proclaims that he is going to

---

[87] On the use of 'Galilaean', see H. Karpp, 'Christennamen', in *RAC* 2. 1131.

convert immediately, and in full view of everyone, 'he flew to the aid of our Galilaean [Christ], and from my own humbleness requested that henceforth he be enrolled under His name' (19. 7). Galilaeus' real name, it appears, has been suppressed in favour of a more 'appropriate' name.[88]

Finally, we can complete our picture of the Jewish gentry by mentioning the families of Caecilianus and Innocentius. Caecilianus is a 'man of rank' (vir honestus) and so 'eminent' (praecipuus) among both Jews and Christians that he had been elected defensor civitatis (19. 6). He is, in fact, the senior civic magistrate in Magona at the time of the conversion in 418. He ranks second in the synagogue after Theodorus (19. 8). He and his brother Florianus are both Fathers of the Jews (patres Iudaeorum), a title well attested in inscriptions from other regions (19. 8).[89] Innocentius, on the other hand, is a refugee who had recently fled the warfare on the Spanish mainland and found refuge on Minorca (18. 4). It is Innocentius who flees to the hills along with Meletius after the disastrous debate at which many Jews wrongly conclude that Theodorus has converted.[90] Meletius addresses Innocentius as 'learned not only in Latin literature, but in Greek literature as well, and meditating constantly on the Law' (18. 15). Innocentius counsels capitulation and acceptance of Christianity, but his wife puts up a stubborn resistance, rejecting for four days his 'threats, prayers, and tears' (27. 2). It is only through the occupation of their house by Severus and some of his flock that this woman can at last be 'persuaded' to convert. Her widowed sister displays an even greater resistance. Severus claims that Innocentius' sister-in-law was the only Jew on the island who, to his knowledge, preferred exile to conversion (28. 9). At the news of Innocentius' conversion, she immediately boarded ship with her two young daughters in order to emigrate (26. 2). On 9 February, however, she returned and begged forgiveness and acceptance in the church for herself and her two girls (28. 3–9).

---

[88] The request to be 'enrolled' under Christ's name refers to being registered among the Christians. It does not appear to me to allude to a genuine name change at conversion. On this latter phenomenon, see G. H. R. Horsley, 'Name Change as an Indication of Religious Conversion in Antiquity', Numen, 34 (1987), 1–17.

[89] On pater/mater as synagogue titles, see Brooten, Women Leaders, 64–72.

[90] Demougeot, 'L'Évêque Sévère' 20 mistakenly takes Meletius and Innocentius to be brothers. The Jews in Ep. Sev., like the Christians, address one another as 'brother'. Note the vocatives Innocenti frater (18. 11), and frater Theodore (19. 9).

The presence of Innocentius and his family raises the interesting problem of refugees in this period. The barbarian invasions produced thousands of refugees, including a number of people already mentioned here: Avitus, Orosius, and Pelagius.[91] Was Innocentius an isolated example or one of many displaced Jews who had settled in Magona, a town obviously receptive to Jews? Severus says nothing on the topic, but there is a curious mention later in the letter of Jews who had been driven to the island and were waiting for favourable sailing weather (23). Why were these Jews risking a mid-winter sea voyage? Were they simply rash or, perhaps, compelled by circumstances?[92] Again, Severus says nothing, but we should be aware of the possibility that warfare on the mainland had produced a stream of refugees in the Balearics, which lay on one of the two routes available to people fleeing Spain by sea.

Despite the invective against Jews as vipers and scorpions, it is clear that Jewish–Christian relations in Magona had been amicable. Severus speaks at 5. 1 of the 'obligation of greeting one another' (salutationis officia), their 'old habit of easy acquaintance' (consuetudo familiaritatis), and the 'sinful appearance of long-standing affection' (noxia inveteratae species caritatis). Magona's Jews were not merely well integrated—they were apparently the dominant social group in the town and their presence was taken for granted, or so we may infer from the allusion to 'our complacency' (tepor noster), which 'heated up' when Stephen's relics arrived on the island (4. 4). When Theodorus finally agreed to convert, the reaction of the Christian crowd was dramatic: 'Some ran to him affectionately and caressed his face and neck with kisses, others embraced him in gentle arms, while still others longed to join right hands with him or to engage him in conversation' (16. 18).

The social prestige of the local Jews clearly had a great impact on Magona's social and political life, but did the prestige of the synagogue leaders also affect the religious life of Magona's Christians? Severus claims that 'Magona seethed with so great a multitude of Jews, as if with vipers and

---

[91] On the many Spanish clergy who fled their posts, see P. Courcelle, Histoire littéraire des grandes invasions germaniques (Paris, 1964), 67, 97.

[92] On winter sailing in the Mediterranean, see J. Rougé, 'La Navigation hivernale sous l'empire romain', REA 54 (1952), 316–25.

scorpions, that Christ's church was being wounded by them daily' (3. 6: *Magona tantis Iudaeorum populis velut colubris scorpionibusque fervebat, ut quotidie ab his Christi ecclesia morderetur*). Although the island's vipers and scorpions are non-poisonous, according to Severus, the Jews with their 'lethal poison of unbelief' have inflicted considerable harm on the town of Magona. He does not clarify how his Christian flock was being harmed by their Jewish neighbours, with whom they clearly enjoyed cordial relations, but it is worth considering the possible ways in which the prestige of the synagogue affected the religious practices of local Christians. The synagogue building itself appears to be in town (cf. 12. 7–13. 3), whereas the church is in an isolated spot outside the town (20. 4), and the superior wealth of the synagogue leaders undoubtedly ensured that the synagogue was the more impressive edifice. Theodorus, the synagogue's Father of Fathers, had fulfilled all the town's curial duties and is considered the *patronus*, whereas Severus resides in Jamona and can only come to Magona occasionally. The letter mentions nothing specific about the religious habits of Magona's Jews, apart from the most predictable aspects of Judaism: Sabbath observance, and a synagogue containing silver and holy books (12. 4; 13. 13). But evidence from other provinces reveals the sort of practices Christians might adopt in imitation or admiration of their Jewish neighbours, customs often branded as objectionable by bishops who wished to preserve firm boundaries between the two communities.

The antiquity and sanctity of Jewish customs made a deep impression on many Christians, who, after all, studied the history of ancient Israel, immersed themselves in the stories of its patriarchs and prophets, learned the psalms by heart, and listened to readings from the Jewish holy books every time they entered a church. Some Christians felt that their spiritual life was enhanced by observance of the Sabbath, the annual round of festivals, dietary regulations, and other Jewish ceremonies.[93] Scattered evidence from around the empire, particularly in the fourth century, reveals clearly that many religious people simply did not accept the orthodox insistence on the mainten-

[93] For a general survey of Jewish observances, see S. Safrai, 'Religion in Everyday Life', in *CRINT* 2. 793–833.

ance of firm, high boundaries between Jews and Christians.[94] Church canons from the period reveal the sorts of issues that troubled church authorities. The bishops at Elvira (c.300/13) forbade Jewish–Christian intermarriage (Canon 16), the blessing of the fields by Jews (Canon 49), eating with Jews (Canon 50), and adultery with Jewish women (Canon 78).[95] At the Council of Antioch (341), the assembled bishops prohibited eating with Jews at Passover (Canon 1).[96] The Canons of Laodicea (360?) prohibited rest on the Sabbath (Canon 29), the celebration of Jewish festivals, particularly the acceptance of gifts from Jews during their festivals (Canon 37), and eating unleavened bread at Passover (Canon 38).[97]

These issues are also apparent from the anti-Jewish polemic of the age, particularly the series of eight sermons preached in Antioch by John Chrysostom in 386–7. Although entitled *Against the Jews*, they are really directed against 'Judaizing' Christians in his congregation who have allowed themselves to be drawn into a whole range of Jewish practices, particularly observance of the annual cycle of festivals: the autumn New Year celebration, the day of Atonement, and Tabernacles, as well as the spring festival of Passover. The vituperation of these speeches in no way obscures the evidence they provide for day-to-day contact and mutual influence between Christians and Jews. The well-known incident of oath swearing in a synagogue illustrates the problem for a local bishop. Chrysostom describes how he 'rescued' a Christian woman who was being 'dragged' into a synagogue by a fellow Christian to formalize a business deal by swearing an oath. He upbraided the man for his 'stupidity', accusing him of being 'no better than a jackass' if he thought he could worship Christ and drag someone into the 'haunts of the Jews'. To his infuriated demand for an explanation, the man replied simply that 'many people' had told him that oaths sworn in synagogues 'inspired more fear'.[98]

[94] A. M. Rabello, 'L'Observance des fêtes juives dans l'empire romain', in *ANRW* 19 (1980), 1288–1312.

[95] C. J. Hefele and H. Leclercq (edd.), *Histoire des Conciles*, i (Paris, 1907), 212–64.

[96] Ibid. 714.

[97] Ibid. 1015–19.

[98] *Adv. Iudaeos* 1. 3 (*PG* 48. 847–8). Cf. M. Simon, 'La Polémique antijuive de saint Jean Chrysostome et le mouvement judaïsant d'Antioche', in id., *Recherches d'Histoire Judéo-Chrétienne* (Paris, 1962), 140–53; W. Meeks and R. Wilken, *Jews and Christians in Antioch in the First Four Centuries of the Common Era* (Missoula, Mont., 1978), 90–1. The

From anecdotes such as this as well as the evidence of the Canons, a picture emerges of Jews and Christians living side by side in the cramped quarters of ancient towns, greeting one another in the street, entering one another's shops, and occasionally participating in one another's religious customs and festivals.[99]

Judaizing resists easy definition because it often occurs on commonly owned ground between firmly defined religious camps.[100] The Judaizing of our oath-swearer, for example, may have been quite minimal—perhaps confined to business deals. Some Judaizers, however, like the well-attested 'God-fearers', manifested an intense interest and participation in Jewish life without having taken the last step to full conversion.[101] Emperors did not generally meddle in such matters, but they showed serious concern over the full conversion of Christians to Judaism. For example, Jewish ownership of non-Jewish slaves posed a constant problem, since some tasks in a Jewish household could only be performed by a Jew. Certainly, full participation in the religious life of the household was only possible for Jews, and Jewish law required non-Jewish slaves to convert to Judaism and, if male, to undergo circumcision. Slaves provided a steady stream of converts to Judaism. Jewish rule over Christians, however, was, from the Christian perspective, unacceptable, and prompted a long and intense effort by Roman emperors to prohibit Jews from owning or acquiring non-Jewish slaves, since it was all but inevitable that they would be converted.[102]

How much of all this had been taking place on Minorca cannot be known, but, in light of the prominence of the local

sermons are translated in P. W. Harkins, *Saint John Chrysostom, Discourses against Judaizing Christians* (The Fathers of the Church, 68; Washington, D.C., 1979).

[99] On the attraction of Judaism, see R. L. Wilken, *John Chrysostom and the Jews: Rhetoric and Reality in the Late 4th Century* (Berkeley, 1983), 66–94; L. H. Feldman, *Jew and Gentile in the Ancient World: Attitudes and Interactions from Alexander to Justinian* (Princeton, 1992), 177–287, 369–82.

[100] On Judaizers in the early church, see M. Simon, *Verus Israel A Study of the Relations between Christians and Jews in the Roman Empire (135–425)* (Eng. tr.: Oxford, 1986), 306–38; Feldman, *Jew and Gentile in the Ancient World*, 177–287.

[101] On God-fearers, see J. Reynolds and R. Tannenbaum, *Jews and Godfearers at Aphrodisias* (Cambridge Philological Society Supplementary, 12; Cambridge, 1987); Feldman, *Jew and Gentile in the Ancient World*, 342–82.

[102] A. Linder (ed.), *The Jews in Roman Imperial Legislation* (Detroit, 1987), 82–5.

Jews, we can easily imagine the possible ways in which 'Christ's church was being wounded by them daily.' The 'little world' of Minorca was visited in good sailing weather by sea traffic making its way between Spain and North Africa, Italy, and Gaul. But from October to March, there would have been little activity in the ports, apart from ships making the short run over to Majorca. In a small, relatively isolated town like Magona, religious groups could not easily avoid one another and it is hardly surprising that they exchanged customary greetings and maintained a habit of easy familiarity with one another. It would not be surprising either if Magona's Christians participated in some Jewish customs and holidays. This would be all the more likely in Magona, given the social and political prominence of the leaders of the synagogue. The simple fact that the patronage network in Magona began with the head of the synagogue would have had far-reaching implications for the general prestige of the Jewish minority and their interaction with the Christian majority.

## VI. THE MILLENNIUM AND THE CONVERSION OF THE JEWS

In the 'face-to-face' environment of Magona, people had to live with the consequences of their actions. There was no anonymity in such towns. How then do we explain how one religious group could bring itself to terrorize with the threat of death neighbours with whom they had apparently lived in harmony, particularly when the leaders of the religious 'enemy' wielded enormous social and political clout? Three issues need to be explored: (1) the role of Stephen's relics, (2) the letter's allusions to the millennium and the conversion of the Jews, and (3) Severus' own views on religious coercion. I will examine the first two issues here and reserve the third for the following section. First, the presence of Stephen's relics. Severus implies that religious fervour leading to confrontation broke out almost instantaneously after the relics were placed in Magona's church: 'straightaway (*protinus*) the fire of His love was kindled. . . . Immediately (*statim*) our complacency heated up' (4. 3–4). As the drama unfolds, however, Stephen recedes into the background and plays only a minor role. Severus has made no mention of a formal *adventus* of the relics and he does not appear very interested in the management of Stephen's cult. In fact, he will mention the saint only three more times in the letter (6. 4; 20. 4, 12), and only one of those passages accords Stephen a prominent role (6. 4). Although a stone-throwing riot breaks out at 13. 3, Severus passes up the opportunity to draw a parallel with Stephen's lapidation. But no passage reveals more clearly Severus' relative lack of interest in Stephen than the incident in which a miraculous ball of light descends over the Christian basilica outside Magona. Severus concludes: 'But it is still today unclear whether this thing was an angel or St Stephen himself or what it really appeared to be' (20. 12). Severus' interest in Stephen is quite specific. Stephen, as John of Jerusalem observed, was the 'first to wage the Lord's wars against the Jews', and Severus, who became bishop at about the time that the relics arrived, quickly enlisted Stephen as a divine patron in his campaign to rectify the intolerable Jewish dominance of Magona.

As we noted above, the relics had arrived in late summer or autumn 416. The religious tension they allegedly provoked persisted throughout the year 417. On the divine level, this consisted of a struggle between divine patrons: the Maccabees vs. St Stephen (6. 4; 8. 4).[103] On the human level, Theodorus and other Jewish leaders held firm against the new bishop. Severus' narrative appears to preserve hints of the polemical discussions that were going on among the populace. After the outbreak of religious fervour, he claims, 'In every public place, battles were waged against the Jews over the Law, in every house struggles over the faith' (5. 2). We have already cited the 'aged teachers of the Law', who came to believe 'without any verbal wrangling, without any dispute over the Scriptures' (21. 5). This may be an inadvertent allusion to the 'wrangling' and 'disputes' that had gone on in the past year.

The conversion of Minorca's Jews was, as Peter Brown observed, a 'thoroughly dirty business',[104] and yet, surprisingly,

---

[103] On the Maccabees, see C. Rampolla, 'Martyre et sépulture des Machabées,' *Revue de l'art chrétien* 42 (1899), 290–305 (pts. 1–2), 377–92 (pts. 3–5), 457–65 (pt. 6); E. Bikerman, 'Les Maccabées de Malalas', *Byzantion*, 21 (1951), 63–83.

[104] P. Brown, *The Cult of the Saints* (Chicago, 1981), 104.

Severus makes little attempt to deflect responsibility for events on to St Stephen. On the contrary, he exculpates himself and his Christian flock by de-emphasizing his own role and by presenting his congregation as agents of God carrying out a divinely ordered plan for the conversion of the Jews in the last stages of human history. The driving force in the letter is the fiery 'zeal' (*zelus* or *caritas*) felt by Christians who are expecting the millennium:

When this was done, straightaway the fire of His love was kindled, the fire which the Lord came to cast upon the earth [Luke 12: 49] and which He wishes to blaze forth. Immediately our complacency heated up, and, as it is written, our hearts were 'burning by the way' [Luke 24: 32]. At one moment, zeal for the faith would fire our hearts; at another moment, the hope of saving a multitude would spur us on.[105]

In the *Letter*, as in the New Testament, fire is ambiguous, occasionally an image of divine inspiration, but more often an image of violent judgement at the end of time, as in the passage from Luke cited by Severus.[106] The approach of the End will produce strife and discord as people confront the necessary dissolution of conventional human bonds. Not only the laws of civil society, but even the most intimate ties of family must be discarded. That is how Severus wants to understand and justify the 'dirty business' in which he is engaged. On Minorca, the heat of the faith and an expectation of the End overpowered conventional relations between Christians and Jews as 'long-standing affection was transformed into temporary hatred, though for love of eternal salvation' (5. 1).

As we just noted, fire in the *Letter* can be both benign and destructive. Fire burns the synagogue to the ground (13. 13), but it also provides spiritual illumination (14). Later, a miraculous ball of light that descends over Magona's church is compared by Severus to the fiery column that guided the

---

[105] 4. 3–4. Other instances of *zelus*: 13. 6; 31. 2; *caritas*: 4. 3; 31. 4.
[106] Note the benign use of fire at Acts 2: 3–4: 'And there appeared to them tongues as of fire, distributed and resting on each one of them. And they were all filled with the Holy Spirit'; cf. Luke 3: 9, 16; Matt. 13: 40.

ancient Israelites in their wandering through the desert [Ex. 16] (20. 16). From the appearance of this sign, argues Severus:

it may be inferred that Jews throughout the whole world are to be visited with the light of faith, since indeed so great a splendour of heavenly grace has shone upon us, who live on this island and, if I may use the phrase, in 'this little world', so that the revelation of signs should extend to the utmost boundaries of our world.    (20. 20–1)

And at the very end of the letter, he links this new mission to evangelize the Jews to the expectation of the approaching End of the world:

Perhaps that time predicted by the Apostle has indeed now come when the fullness of the Gentiles will have come in and all Israel shall be saved [Rom. 11: 25]. And perhaps the Lord wished to kindle this spark from the ends of the earth so that the whole breadth of the earth might be ablaze with the flame of love in order to burn down the forest of unbelief.    (31. 3–4)

In the final days, all the Gentiles will be converted and the Jews, who have so long resisted the Gospel, will at last themselves be saved.[107] All Christian writers accepted Paul's prediction, although Paul's text cannot be said to figure prominently in early Christian writing.[108] The End and the Jews were important preoccupations of early Christians, but the two issues did not generally converge. Christian writings are more concerned with Jewish error in the present than with the fact that all will be forgiven at the End. Severus has taken the remarkable step of anticipating, rather prematurely, the end of history and the ultimate reconciliation of Jewish and Christian rivals.

Severus' allusions to the End frame the narrative and are

[107] Cf. Rom. 11: 25–9: 'I want you to understand this mystery, brethren: a hardening has come upon part of Israel, until the full number of the Gentiles come in, and so all Israel will be saved. . . . As regards the gospel they are enemies of God, for your sake; but as regards election they are beloved for the sake of their forefathers. For the gifts and the call of God are irrevocable.'

[108] The material is reviewed by F. J. Caubet Iturbe, 'Et sic omnis Israel salvus fieret, Rom. 11: 26. Su interpretación por los escritores cristianos de los siglos III–XII', Estudios bíblicos, 21 (1962), 127–50.

used to justify conduct which, by conventional Roman standards, is flagrantly illegal. But millenarian expectations are not even hinted at in the body of the narrative. Are these expectations genuine, or is St Paul merely a convenient proof text to justify religious coercion that would otherwise be judged unacceptable? Is it significant that Severus hedges his millenarian claim (cf. 31. 3: 'Perhaps (*forsitan*) that time . . . has indeed now come. . . . And perhaps (*fortasse*) the Lord wished . . .')?

It is clear that millenarian expectations were rife in Severus' lifetime. They were of course hardly new. The prominence of Jesus' messianic message, preserved chiefly in the Gospels and John's Revelation, ensured that a concern with the End would remain a permanent feature of Christianity.[109] In the early church, theories about the end of time were frequently linked to the eschatological concept of the cosmic week, or the ages of the world.[110] Putting together the creation account in Genesis with a line from Psalm 89/90 ('A thousand years is as yesterday in the sight of the Lord'), early Christians arrived at the theory of the cosmic week. As the Lord had created the world in six days, so the world would endure for 6,000 years. At the end of the sixth age, the year 6000 after creation, Jesus would return in glory to inaugurate the thousand-year reign of his saints (Rev. 20: 4– 5), after which, in the year 7000, would occur the final End of the world. To know the date of the End, one had simply to calculate the age of the world. Christian chronographers provided the answer, or rather a series of answers, to this pressing problem. The most common theory maintained that Christ was born 5,500 years after the Creation and, hence, the End, that is, the inauguration of the millennium, would happen in the year 500. Once this fascination with knowing the End was unleashed, however, it was difficult to control. There was no

[109] The literature on millenarianism is large. See P. Fredriksen, 'Apocalypse and Redemption in Early Christianity from John of Patmos to Augustine of Hippo', *VChr* 45 (1991), 151–83 (with bibliography).

[110] J. Daniélou, 'La Typologie millénariste de la semaine dans le christianisme primitif', *VChr* 2 (1948), 1–16. There is an exhaustive treatment of chronography and millenarianism in R. Landes, 'Lest the Millennium be Fulfilled: Apocalyptic Expectations and the Pattern of Western Chronography 100–800 C. E.', in W. Verbeke, D. Verhelst, and A. Welkenhuysen (edd.), *The Use and the Abuse of Eschatology in the Middle Ages* (Louvain, 1988), 137–211.

orthodoxy and the year 500 had many competitors, a number of which clustered around 400.[111]

Earthquakes, pestilence of unusual severity, and, most importantly of all, military defeats added to a growing sense in these years that the calamities afflicting the empire were beyond the measure of previous experience and signalled the approach of the End.[112] As Jacques Fontaine wrote, 'en cette fin du IVᵉ siècle ... en Espagne et en Gaule ... [il y eut] une résurgence d'une vie charismatique et d'une attente eschatologique comparables à celle des premiers siècles chrétiens'.[113] Two incidents from the year 398 illustrate the peculiar atmosphere of the period. In his *Sermon on the Sack of the City of Rome*, Augustine relates a story of an event that had occurred in Constantinople in 398.[114] A high official dreamed that the 'city would perish by fire coming from heaven'.[115] His bishop took the dream seriously and began to wait. When the day arrived, a 'fiery cloud' appeared in the East and a 'mighty flame seemed to hang down from heaven'. People wildly sought baptism wherever they could in expectation of the final conflagration. Although the cloud eventually disappeared, another report informed them that the city would be destroyed on the following Sabbath. Led by the emperor (!), the whole city withdrew several miles to wait in anxious prayer, and only after the fateful day had passed did they return to find everything as they had left it. Pagan prophecies predicted the eventual demise of Christianity.[116] In the *City of God*, for example, Augustine recounts the remarkable tale of a pagan oracle which had predicted that Christianity would disappear from the earth in

[111] B. Kötting, 'Endzeitprognosen zwischen Lactantius und Augustinus', *HJ* 77 (1958), 125–39.

[112] The evidence is compiled in Kötting, 'Endzeitprognosen', 123–39; Landes, 'Lest the Millennium be Fulfilled', 155 nn. 68–70a.

[113] J. Fontaine (ed.), *Vita Sancti Martini*, SC 135 (Paris, 1969), 1021.

[114] M. V. O'Reilly (ed.), *Augustine: De Excidio Urbis Romae Sermo* (Patristic Studies, 89; Washington, D.C., 1955), 68–70, with her note on 89.

[115] Cf. Rev. 20: 9–10: 'fire came down from heaven and consumed them, and the devil who had deceived them was thrown into the lake of fire and sulphur where the beast and the false prophet were, and they will be tormented day and night for ever and ever.'

[116] H. Chadwick, 'Oracles of the End in the Conflict of Paganism and Christianity in the Fourth Century', in E. Lucchesi and H. D. Saffrey (edd.), *Mémorial André-Jean Festugière: Antiquité païenne et chrétienne* (Geneva, 1984), 125–9.

the year 398.[117] A Greek oracle described a magic ceremony in which St Peter killed a year-old child (*puer anniculus*) as a foundation sacrifice to ensure the survival of the new religion for 365 years, corresponding to the 365 days of the child's age. Such things were believed by the 'empty-headed', claims Augustine, but nearly thirty years had lapsed since the passing of that fateful year and Christianity had not disappeared. On the contrary, anyone could see that it had grown, 'especially by the conversion of those who were held back from the faith because they took that prophecy to be true'.[118]

Of all the calamities that afflicted Gaul, Spain, and Italy in these years, the sack of Rome in 410 had the most powerful effect on public opinion. Pagans complained bitterly that the empire's collapse was due to the emperors' adoption of Christianity and the abandonment of the old gods, and Christians were hard pressed to find a response. The triumphalism of the age of Theodosius, when Christians marvelled at the spectacular success of their religion, gave way to hesitation and doubt. The 'Christian times' (*tempora Christiana*), which had been the source of pride only a few years before, became the butt of jokes in the years after 410.[119] In his sermons from the years after 410, Augustine often counter-attacked against pagan slander and laboured to bolster faltering Christians, but anxieties about the nature of the times did not quickly disappear.[120]

Spain's political and military troubles in these years can be traced to the invasion of the Western empire that had begun in late 406, when a confederacy of tribes crossed the Rhine near Mainz and set in motion the final disintegration of the Western

[117] *De Civ. Dei* 18. 53–4 (*CSEL* 40(2). 356–62), with G. Bardy (ed.), *Œuvres de Saint Augustin. La Cité de Dieu xv–xviii*, BA 36 (Paris, 1960), 774–5 n. 59. The oracle is discussed by J. Hubaux, 'Saint Augustin et la crise cyclique', in *Augustinus Magister (Congrès international augustinien, Paris 21–24 septembre 1954)*, ii (Paris, 1954), 943–50; id., 'Saint Augustin et la crise eschatologique de la fin du IVe siècle', *BAB* 40 (1954), 658–73.

[118] *De Civ. Dei* 18. 54 (*CSEL* 40(2). 361).

[119] On reaction to the invasions, see Courcelle, *Histoire littéraire des grandes invasions*, *passim*. On the debate over *tempora Christiana* and Augustine's shifting views, see R. A. Markus, *Saeculum: History and Society in the Theology of St. Augustine* (Cambridge, 1970), 22–44; W. H. C. Frend, 'Augustine and Orosius on the End of the Ancient World', *AugStud* 20 (1989), 1–38.

[120] P. Courcelle, 'Propos antichrétiens rapportés par Saint Augustin', *Recherches augustiniennes*, i (1958), 149–86, esp. 177–83; F. Paschoud, *Roma Aeterna: Etudes sur le patriotisme romain dans l'occident latin à l'époque des grandes invasions* (Rome, 1967), 239–45.

Roman Empire and with it the end of Roman rule in Spain.[121] For the next three years (407–9) these tribes peregrinated through the Gauls, leaving in their wake devastation, famine, and political chaos. The provinces of Spain could do little but wait 'trembling' at the thought of what lay in store for them.[122] Usurpers quickly took advantage of the confusion to set up short-lived kingdoms in Gaul and Spain and made it all the more difficult for the government in Ravenna to mount any serious resistance. The usurpers in Spain successfully crushed the attempt of kinsmen of the Emperor Honorius to hold the provinces for the legitimate emperor, but they proved incapable of opposing the barbarians.[123] In late September 409 the confederacy of tribes breached the passes of the Pyrenees unopposed. The federated barbarian troops who had been stationed to guard the passes apparently made no effort to stop the invaders, preferring instead to join them in the slaughter and devastation of the Spanish provinces in the years 410 and 411. The Spanish chronicler Hydatius describes the effects of the invasions in apocalyptic imagery recalling Ezekiel:

As barbarians ran riot through Spain and an evil plague raged no less fiercely, the tyrannical tax-collector stole and the soldiery exhausted the wealth and provisions stored in the cities. So severe was the famine that people devoured human flesh in their violent hunger. Mothers killed, cooked, and ate the bodies of their own children. Wild beasts became accustomed to the corpses of men killed by the sword, famine, and plague. They even killed strong men and fed on their flesh, unleashing death everywhere against the human race. And so, as the four plagues of iron, hunger, pestilence, and wild beasts raged everywhere in the world, the predictions announced by the Lord through his prophets were fulfilled.[124]

[121] On the Germanic invasions, see J. B. Bury, *History of the Later Roman Empire*, i (New York, 1958), 174–209; L. Musset, *The Germanic Invasions* (Eng. tr.: University Park, Penn., 1975), 30–66.

[122] Jer. *Ep.* 123. 15 (*CSEL* 56. 92): *ipsae Hispaniae iam iamque periturae cotidie contremescunt recordantes inruptionis Cymbricae . . . et quicquid alii* [the Gauls] *semel passi sunt, illae semper timore patiuntur.*

[123] Oros. *Hist.* 7. 40. 4–10; Olympiod. fr. 13 (ed. Blockley).

[124] Hydatius, *Chron.* 48 (*s.a.* 410); Olympiod. fr. 29. 2 (ed. Blockley), also reports famine so severe that acts of cannibalism took place, cf. Ezek. 14: 21: 'These were the words of the Lord, "How much less hope is there for Jerusalem when I inflict on her

Spain in these years was virtually abandoned by the Roman government at Ravenna. The Emperor Honorius could not mount an effective resistance to the invasion of Italy, much less far-off Spain. The Spaniards Orosius and Hydatius probably reflect the popular perception at the time when they report that the invaders simply divided up the country 'by lot' and settled down in the provinces which they had drawn.[125] Only Tarraconensis in the east of the country remained, in name at least, under Roman rule.

For three years (412–15), the provinces of Spain enjoyed a respite from open warfare. In 415, however, the Roman general Constantius drove the Visigoths under King Wallia out of Gaul down into Spain, where they, and the civilian population, were slowly starved by a naval blockade. In the following year, Wallia reached an agreement with the Roman government by which he, as a Roman federate, would make war on behalf of Rome against the tribes who had occupied the peninsula in 410–11. Once again, the provinces were engulfed in warfare, from 416 until early 418, when the Roman government suddenly recalled Wallia and negotiated the settlement of the Visigoths in southern Gaul, leaving Spain largely in the control of what was left of the original invaders.[126] It was this last round of fighting that prevented Orosius from returning to his native Galicia. Throughout these years, the inhabitants of the Balearics anxiously waited, uncertain whether calamity would overwhelm them as well. In fact, the islands would be spared until 425.[127]

To conclude, expectations of the End were a conspicuous feature of the religious atmosphere of the period and it is plausible that Severus and his flock would be susceptible to them. Anxiety about the End was not, in my view, the dominant motive for Severus, since millenarian ideas do not play a significant role in the narrative itself. But millenarianism

---

these four punishments of mine, sword and famine, wild beasts and pestilence, to destroy both men and cattle!"'

[125] Hydatius, *Chron.* 49 (*s.a.* 411): *sorte ad inhabitandum sibi provinciarum dividunt regiones*; Oros. *Hist.* 8. 40. 10: *habita sorte et distributa usque ad nunc possessione consistunt.*

[126] E. A. Thompson, 'The Settlement of the Barbarians in Southern Gaul', *JRS* 46 (1956), 65–75.

[127] Hydatius, *Chron.* 86 (*s.a.* 425): *Vandali Baliaricas insulas depraedantur.*

provided an intellectual framework in which the deliberate provocation of communal violence could be understood and in some sense justified. Social upheaval and the salvation of the Jews would both occur in the last days. Admittedly, the millenarianism of Minorca's Christians took a remarkable form, since they applied in practice a prediction about the End and the Jews that was held to apply to a far-distant future. Moreover, Severus would have received scant support for this point of view from the dominant churchmen of his day. Augustine, for example, had always deplored attempts to calculate the end of the world and the inclination to interpret present evils as signs of the approaching End. He became even less sympathetic to such tendencies in his later years.[128] His fullest critique of millenarianism is found in an exchange of letters with Bishop Hesychius of Salona dating precisely from the year 418.[129] Nor would Orosius have served as a catalyst to spark a millenarian outbreak, since he reacted to pagan criticism of 'Christian times' by denying that anything was wrong. Augustine had intended that Orosius' *History* demonstrate the folly of interpreting the events of secular history as 'signs' of salvation history, but Orosius, intentionally or unintentionally, missed the point. He took a providential view of Roman history, stressing the link between the coming of Christ and the foundation of the empire, and interpreting the establishment of a Christian empire as the unfolding of God's plan.[130] His response to present disaster was polemical denial. Times had never been better: 'I would permit Christian times to be blamed freely, if, from the founding of the world to the present, any equally

---

[128] See G. Folliet, 'La Typologie du *sabbat* chez Saint Augustin. Son interprétation millénariste entre 389 et 400', *REAug* 2 (1956), 371–90. G. Bonner, 'Augustine and Millenarianism', in R. Williams (ed.), *The Making of Orthodoxy: Essays in Honour of Henry Chadwick* (Cambridge, 1989), 235–54.

[129] *Epp.* 197–9. The contents of the letters are reviewed by J.-P. Bouhot, 'Hesychius de Salone et Augustin', in A.-M. La Bonnardière (ed.), *Saint Augustin et la Bible* (Paris, 1986), 229–50.

[130] On Orosius' providentialism and his relations with Augustine, see T. E. Mommsen, 'Orosius and Augustine', in E. F. Rice (ed.), *Medieval and Renaissance Studies* (Ithaca, NY, 1959), 325–48; H. I. Marrou, 'Saint Augustin, Orose et l'augustinisme historique', *La storiografia altomedievale*, vol. 1 (Settimane di Studio del Centro Italiano di Studi sull'Alto Medioevo 17, 10–16 aprile 1969; Spoleto, 1970), 59–87; F. Paschoud, 'La polemica provvidenzialistica di Orosio', *La storiografia ecclesiastica nella tarda antichità* (Atti del convegno tenuto in Erice, 3–8 dicembre 1978; Messina, 1980), 113–33.

fortunate period can be pointed out.'[131] If Severus was prone to see signs of the End in present events in Spain, he will not have found a sympathetic listener in Orosius.


## VII. SEVERUS AND CONSENTIUS ON THE COERCION OF JEWS AND HERETICS

### a) *Orthodoxy and Religious Coercion in the Fourth and Fifth Centuries*

Although the linking of expectations of the End and the salvation of the Jews was exceptional, the means used to coerce the Jews towards salvation were all too familiar. Events on Minorca fit a pattern that became disturbingly predictable in the later fourth and early fifth centuries, especially in the Eastern empire where Jewish communities were more common and tensions between Christians and Jews more pronounced. In this period, synagogues were burned or converted into churches in an impressive number of cities: Callinicus, Stobi, Apamea, Edessa, Alexandria, Antioch, Tipasa (Algeria), Rome, Aquileia, and Magona.[132] In the years just before the mass conversion on Minorca, there are well-attested instances of anti-Jewish rioting. The Byzantine chronicler Agapius (d. 941) reports that in 411, some Jews who had been forcibly baptized mocked the Christians by crucifying a statue of Christ and crying out, 'That is your Messiah!' The result was religious rioting.[133] In 414, Cyril of Alexandria is alleged to have expelled the large Jewish community from Alexandria, and he did so under the very nose of the Prefect Orestes, who had sided with the Jews in an ongoing Jewish–Christian dispute.[134] Jews were not always passive victims in these affairs, particularly in towns

---

[131] *Hist.* 7. 43. 16.

[132] For a full dossier of anti-Jewish riots in this period, see J. Juster, *Les Juifs dans l'empire romain*, i (Paris, 1914), 464 n. 3; L. Cracco Ruggini, 'Ebrei e orientali nell'Italia settentrionale fra il IV e il VI secolo d. Cr.', *SDHI* 25 (1959), 205–7; Simon, *Verus Israel*, 264–74; E. D. Hunt, 'St. Stephen in Minorca: An Episode in Jewish–Christian Relations in the Early 5th Century AD', *JThS* NS 33 (1982), 116–17.

[133] Agapius, *Chronicle* (*PO* 8. 408).

[134] Socrates, *HE* 7. 13 (*PG* 67. 760). It is unclear how we should interpret Socrates' evidence, since it is unlikely that Cyril could successfully expel a large and economically important ethnic group.

where they were a sizeable minority. It was apparently not uncommon for Jews, in the words of one imperial law, to 'become insolent and, elated by their own security, commit some rash act in disrespect of the Christian religion'.[135] A law of 408 instructs governors to forbid Jews at their annual festival of Purim to burn the effigy of Haman (who was hung on a cross) 'in contempt of Christian religion'.[136] Socrates recounts an incident from Inmestar (between Antioch and Chalcis) which suggests the sort of sport Jews made on Purim. In 414, some drunken Jews, intent on having some fun at the expense of Christianity, hung a Christian boy on a cross and made no secret of who they thought they were crucifying. Unfortunately, the boy died from his rough treatment, which provoked rioting and the intervention of the provincial governor.[137]

A spate of imperial letters from these years attests the unsettling frequency of disturbances involving Jews and Christians. *CTh* 16. 8. 9 (393) reproves the 'excesses of those persons who, in the name of the Christian religion, presume to commit certain unlawful acts and attempt to destroy and to despoil the synagogues'. *CTh* 16. 8. 12 (397) forbids insults to Jews and directs that their synagogues shall remain *in quiete solita*. *CTh* 16. 8. 20 (412) again forbids anyone to 'violate or occupy a synagogue', while 16. 8. 21 from the same year commands that Jews not be subjected to insults and 'their synagogues and habitations shall not be burned indiscriminately'. *CTh* 16. 8. 25 (423) reaffirms that 'no synagogue of the Jews shall be indiscriminately taken away from them or consumed by fire', but it simultaneously recognizes such acts as a *fait accompli* and directs that compensation be made in cases where the site or the building has been consecrated for use as a Christian church. It also forbids the Jews to build any new synagogues. *CTh* 16. 8. 26–7 (423) reasserts the sanctions against 'those persons who commit many rash acts under the pretext of venerable Christianity' as well as the ban on building new synagogues. The very repetition of these laws indicates the recurrence of the problem and suggests that the court is increasingly unable in the early fifth century to control the

---

[135]  *CTh* 16. 8. 21 (412).
[136]  *CTh* 16. 8. 18 (408).
[137]  Socrates, *HE* 7. 16 (*PG* 67. 769).

passions being unleashed in communities around the empire. The emperors themselves contribute to this ominous atmosphere by their refusal or inability to take a firm stand on the status of the Jews.[138] The laws in *CTh* 16. 8 offer a glimpse of emperors attempting to balance the demands of different constituencies, at one moment acceding to anti-Jewish pressure by threatening or revoking certain Jewish rights, while at another moment reaffirming traditional privileges and denouncing outright, physical assault.

Because of the rebellions in Palestine in the early empire, the Jews had long had a reputation for unruliness and sedition, but that reputation took a peculiar twist under Christian emperors, since the charge of killing Christ, which had once been a strictly religious crime, could now be construed as political treachery, for Christ was now the divine guardian of the imperial house. In the early fifth century, Jews were barred from any form of political or military service, a disability justified by equating religious error with political treachery. In 438 Theodosius II reaffirmed these rulings on the grounds that 'it is wrong that persons hostile to the Supernal Majesty and to the Roman laws' should pose as defenders of those laws.[139]

Other developments in Christian thought contributed to the social marginalization of the Jews. Christians of the early empire thought of their world as divided among three peoples: Romans, Jews, and Christians. Developing an idea that the Jews had originally applied to Israel (cf. Zech. 13: 8–9 and Isa. 19: 24), early Christians thought of themselves as the 'third race', an alien people estranged from and in conflict with both Romans and Jews. With their triumph in the fourth century, however, Catholic Christians came to identify themselves with the Romans and to redefine the 'three races' as the three groups of religious outsiders in late Roman society: pagans, heretics, and Jews.[140] Thus, what had been in the early empire

---

[138] On the legal standing of the Jews at this period, see J. Cohen, 'Roman Imperial Policy Toward the Jews from Constantine until the End of the Palestinian Patriarchate (ca. 429)', *ByzStud* 3 (1976), 1–29; B. S. Bachrach, 'The Jewish Community of the Later Roman Empire as seen in the *Codex Theodosianus*', in J. Neusner and E. S. Frerichs (edd.), *'To See Ourselves as Others See Us': Christians, Jews, and 'Others' in Late Antiquity* (Chico, Calif., 1985), 399–421.     [139] *Nov. Theod.* 3. 2.

[140] L. Cracco Ruggini, 'Pagani, ebrei e cristiani: Odio sociologico e odio teologico nel mondo antico', in *Gli ebrei nell'alto medioevo*, i (Settimane di Studio del Centro Italiano di Studi sull'Alto Medioevo 26, 30 marzo–5 aprile 1978; Spoleto, 1980), 15–117.

a 'tripartite dialogue' among the empire's three great religious traditions became in the fourth and fifth centuries a 'tripartite persecution' of all non-Catholics.[141] Religious intolerance and the threat of coercion were facts of life in the period. For Jews, this meant that the relatively favourable status which they had secured from early Roman emperors deteriorated during the course of the fourth century, particularly from the reign of Theodosius I onward.

The presence of a common enemy drove these religious outsiders, pagans, heretics, and Jews, into occasional alliances against Catholics.[142] Pagans and Jews together were responsible for the burning of Christian basilicas during the pagan revival of Julian the Apostate.[143] In conflicts with Catholics in Alexandria, pagan governors had on more than one occasion encouraged an alliance of pagans and Jews. In 373, for example, pagans and Jews had, at the instigation of the governor, succeeded in driving Peter, the new bishop of Alexandria, from his see, temporarily at least.[144] In 408, Jews took part in Donatist attacks against Catholic churches in North Africa.[145] Jews and Arians also might find themselves offering one another mutual support in some instances.[146] In 381, for example, when the Arian Palladius of Ratiaria was anathematized by the Council of Aquileia, he rejected the decision and countered with the suggestion that the doctrinal issues under discussion be judged by pagan *honorati* and Jewish experts in the Old Testament. Ambrose, understandably, rejected the suggestion with contempt.[147]

Although there is no evidence that Jews, pagans, or heretics ever assisted or genuinely welcomed the barbarian invaders of the early fifth century, Catholics might understandably feel uneasy, since none of the invaders of 406 were orthodox Christians.[148] The tribes who invaded Spain in 409 were still pagan,

---

[141] L. Cracco Ruggini, 'Intolerance: Equal and Less Equal in the Roman World', *CPhil* 82 (1987), 201.

[142] Cracco Ruggini, 'Ebrei e orientali' 204–6.

[143] Ambrose, *Ep.* 40. 15 (*PL* 16. 1154).

[144] Theodoret, *HE* 4. 21 (*GCS* 44. 246–7).     [145] *CTh* 16. 5. 44 (408).

[146] Evidence assembled in Cracco Ruggini, 'Ebrei e orientali', 206 n. 46.

[147] L. Cracco Ruggini, 'Tolleranza e intolleranza nella società tardoantica: il caso degli ebrei', *Ricerche di storia sociale e religiosa*, 23 (1983), 31.

[148] But note the comment of Oros. *Hist.* 7. 41. 7 that some Spaniards preferred barbarian overlords to Roman tax-collectors.

and the Goths, who were driven from Gaul into Spain in 415 and then warred against the tribes already settled there, were Arian Christians. The conversion of the Vandals in Spain between 409 and 417, if it genuinely happened, was to Arianism, not to orthodox Catholicism.[149] Moreover, the Arian kingdoms which would rule Spain in the fifth and sixth centuries practised a religious tolerance uncharacteristic of the House of Theodosius that had preceded them or the Catholic kingdoms that would follow them. Jews and heretics fared much better under heretical Arian kings.[150]

## b) *The Literary Collaboration of Severus and Consentius*

It is against this background of uncertainty that we must view Severus' contribution to the contemporary debate over religious coercion, for the *Epistula Severi* is, in effect, a contribution to the debate over 'hard' and 'soft' treatment of Jews. Severus explicitly exhorts his fellow bishops to imitate Christ's zeal, that is, to imitate his own implementation of the 'hard' option (31. 2). Severus is certainly not alone, however, in his support for the 'hard' option in the treatment of the unorthodox. The views of his contemporary Consentius are of particular interest to us, since we know that Consentius actually contributed to the composition of the *Epistula Severi*. The extent of that contribution needs to be investigated. Consentius has long been known from three letters (*Epp.* 119–20, 205) and a treatise *Contra Mendacium* in the corpus of Augustine. But the publication of *Letters* 11* and 12* in the Divjak corpus, both sent to Augustine in 419, has greatly expanded our knowledge of his personality and activities.[151] Consentius emerges from these new letters as a

---

[149] On the conversion of the Vandals, see E. A. Thompson, 'Christianity and the Northern Barbarians', in A. D. Momigliano, *The Conflict Between Paganism and Christianity in the Fourth Century* (Oxford, 1963), 69–71 .

[150] Thompson, *Romans and Barbarians*, 232.

[151] The best treatment of Consentius is found in R. Van Dam, '"Sheep in Wolves' Clothing": The Letters of Consentius to Augustine', *JEH* 37 (1986), 515–35; see also the articles in *Les Lettres de Saint Augustin découvertes par Johannes Divjak, communications présentées au colloque des 20 et 21 septembre 1981* (Paris, 1983): M. Moreau, 'Lecture de la Lettre 11* de Consentius à Augustin', 215–23; J. Wankenne, 'La Correspondance de Consentius avec Saint Augustin', 225–42; H. Marti, 'Citations de Térence: Problèmes et significations des exemples de la Lettre 12* de Consentius à Augustin', 243–9.

puzzling and, to more than one scholar, an irritating personality.[152] In *Letter* 12*, for example, he affects the persona of a world-weary man of *paideia* isolated among rustics in the Balearics, remarking to Augustine on the difficulty on the islands of finding 'I shall not say a learned Christian, but any kind of Christian' (12*. 4. 1). No one of his acquaintance could engage in serious intellectual discussion and it is hard to imagine that he had much respect for Minorca's bishop: 'It is impossible to find even now in these islands—I shall not say someone who teaches great things and clarifies murky issues, but even someone who understands little things and gives some thought to unclouded issues—. . . ' (12*. 5. 1).

Although zealous to take up the pen in religious controversy, Consentius appears intellectually lazy and disinclined to read the works of friend and foe alike. He had acquired Augustine's *Confessions* in about 407, but had set it down after two or three pages, put off by its 'annoying splendour' (*molestus splendor*). He actually began to read the work in 415 (12*. 1. 3). He had compiled a library of 'almost all' the works written against Pelagius, but it was 'still unopened' (12*. 16. 2). That did not deter him, however, from writing on Pelagius, against whom he was at the present moment 'hammering out' his fourth book (12*. 16. 1). He mentions various other works he had composed: a piece against the presbyter Leontius, otherwise unknown (12*. 3. 1), 'two negligible volumes' on an uncertain topic (12*. 5. 2), an anti-Priscillianist tract for Patroclus of Arles (11*. 1. 1), and 'twelve chapters against the Jews' (12*. 15. 2).

He had managed to read Lactantius and the Bible through once (12*. 2. 2), and at 12*. 13. 4 he describes a new resolution that he has taken, namely to begin a reading programme in the Scriptures and to refrain from taking up his pen, even for the purpose of personal correspondence. His new resolution was, however, soon disrupted by Severus:[153]

---

[152] On his personality, note the reaction of E. Dutoit, 'Remarques philologiques et critiques', in *Les Lettres de Saint Augustin* 37, remarking that *Ep.* 12* 'allie l'impertinence, sinon l'insolence, au pédantisme et à la grandiloquence'; also, the characterization of *Ep.* 12* in Van Dam, '"Sheep in Wolves' Clothing"', 526: a 'long-winded defence of his life of retirement, a self-serving (and self-deluding) justification for his lethargy in his study of theology and a presumptuous attempt to elicit praise from Augustine for the few theological tracts he had managed to write'.

[153] J. Wankenne in J. Divjak (ed.), *Œuvres de Saint Augustin*, BA 46B (Paris, 1987),

having in mind this resolution (*propositi*), that I peruse without
great toil the Holy Scriptures alone, but that I abandon my
own writings (if it could be done) even in the form of letters to
acquaintances. . . . It happened at that same time that certain
miraculous things were performed among us at the bidding of
the Lord. When the blessed priest, the brother of your
Paternity, Bishop Severus, along with others who had been
present, had recounted these things to me, by the great force of
his love he broke down my resolution (*irrupit propositum meum*)
and he borrowed from me words alone in order that he himself
might write a letter containing a narrative of the events (*ut
epistolam quae rei gestae ordinem contineret ipse conscriberet, sola a me
verba mutuatus est*).   (12*. 13. 3–6)

But how would Augustine have understood 'he borrowed from
me words alone' or, perhaps, 'he only borrowed from me some
words' (*sola a me verba mutuatus est*)? Severus himself informs us
that he had a multitude of episodes that he could have included
(29. 3). He apparently reserved for himself the choice of what to
include and what to reject. Thus, *sola . . . verba* may mean
'words and phrases, but no more than that' and may be
intended to contrast choice of diction with the selection of
episodes and the overall structure of the narrative, but Consentius could certainly have made himself clearer.

  None the less, a comparison of the two men's works bears
out Consentius' claim of literary collaboration, since there are
numerous verbal parallels, particularly between the *Epistula
Severi* and Consentius' remarkable account in *Epistula* 11* of
the monk Fronto's undercover operation against Priscillianists
on the Spanish mainland. Individually, the parallels may not
be particularly striking, but their cumulative weight suggests
that a number of images or turns of phrase in the *Epistula Severi*

249–51 assumes that Consentius had decided to compose his own narrative on the
conversion of the Jews, but that Severus prevented him (*irrupit propositum meum* = 'il
prévint mon projet') and insisted on writing the narrative himself. He deduces this
meaning of *propositum* from the zeal for composition displayed by Consentius throughout the letter (cf. p. 492, 'en proie à sa rage habituelle d'écrire'). But *propositum* at l. 252
(= 12*. 13. 6) refers to the use of *propositum* above at l. 238 (= 12*. 13. 3), and the *propositum* in the previous sentence is precisely a resolution *not* to write. There is no implica-
tion in the passage that Consentius intended to write a narrative about the conversion
or that Severus had to warn him off his turf. Amengual i Batle, *Els orígens del cristianisme*,
i. 211–13 correctly interprets the *propositum*.

are to be attributed to the intervention of Consentius. The following examples are taken from the more complete list of parallels compiled by Josep Amengual i Batle:[154]

a) Imagery of fiery zeal:

Severus

> *ille, quem Dominus 'venit mittere in terram' [Lc 12: 49] et quem valde ardere cupit, caritatis eius ignis accensus est. Statim siquidem tepor noster incaluit et factum est cor nostrum, sicut scriptum est, 'ardens in via' [Lc 24: 32]* (4. 3–4)
>
> *fidei flamma corripuit* (7. 2)
>
> *Et fortasse hanc ab extremo terrae scintillam voluit Dominus excitari, ut universus orbis terrarum caritatis flagraret incendio ad exurendam infidelitatis silvam* (31. 4)

Consentius

> *Fronto cui spiritus sanctus flagrantissimas fidelis zeli suggerit flammas* (*Ep.* 11\*. 1. 2)
>
> *cum intimis malae conscientiae ignibus ureretur* [Syagrius] (14. 3)
>
> *episcopi Gallicani . . . zeli igne succensi fortasse . . . per omnes provincias uniformis sententiae cauteribus amputetur* (24. 3)
>
> *desiderium flagrantissimis otiandi amoribus praetulisset* (*Ep.* 12\*. 7. 2)
>
> *otii mei ignis exaestuat* (7. 4)
>
> *ignita cauteria* (8. 1)
>
> *talia fomentum verborum amoris nostri ignibus suggerebat* (12. 3)
>
> *solum desidiae anhelabat ardorem* (13. 2)
>
> *desiderii viribus ardentius appetantur* (13. 5)
>
> *ad scribendum furore succensi* (16. 2)

b) Imagery of picnicking in the country

Severus

> *famulorum Christi multitudo . . . iucundius transvolaret quam si ad suburbanum aliquod amoenissimum ad convivia epulari vocaretur* (12. 1–2)

Consentius

> *qui eadem die ad suburbanum profectus iucunde quidem epulatus est* (*Ep.* 11\*. 13. 3)

---

[154] Amengual i Batle, *Els orígens del cristianisme*, i. 204–11. On the literary styles of Consentius and Severus, see also Wankenne, 'La correspondance de Consentius', 225–42; Wankenne and Hambenne, 'La Lettre-encyclique de Severus', 25–6.

c) Jews and heretics as snakes carrying a lethal disease
 Severus
   *colubri . . . velut colubris*   (3. 4–6)
   *mortiferum illud virus incredulitatis abiecerit*   (3. 7)
 Consentius
   *mortiferum virus coluber Severus inseruit*   (*Ep.* 11\*. 11. 4)
   *catholicae fidei quam ignorare mortiferum est*   (*Ep.* 12\*. 4. 1)
   *mortiferum virus* [of Pelagius and Caelestius]   (16. 1)

d) Judaism and heresy as a *pravum iter*
 Severus
   *errore pravi itineris* (= Judaism) *derelicto*   (19. 8)
 Consentius
   *velut comitem pravi itineris* (= Christological error) *increpare*   (*Ep.* 119. 6)

e) Use of the adjective *delibutus*
 Severus
   *aquam mellis sapore delibutam*   (24. 8)
 Consentius
   *illud illecebrosa dulcedine delibutum*   (Ep. *12\**. 9. 3)

f) Use of the expression *non dico . . . sed*
 Severus
   *non dico abstulit sed nec cogitavit diripere*   (13. 12)
 Consentius
   *non dicam doctum, sed vel fideliter Christianum*   (Ep. *12\**. 4. 1)
   *non dicam qui magna doceat et nebulosa dilucidet, sed vel qui parva intelligat et serena dilucidet*   (5. 1)

g) Use of the expression *nemo ferme . . . qui non*
 Severus
   *Nemo enim ferme eorum erat qui non se palam sensisse Christi potentiam contestaretur*   (19. 2)
 Consentius
   *ut nemo ferme hominum . . . inveniri posset qui non me dignum morte decerneret*   (*Ep.* 11\*. 12. 4)

h) Use of the expression *ad auxilium convolare*
 Severus
   *ad matrem propinquam cursu praepeti convolassem*   (11. 5)
   *ad Galilaei nostri convolaret auxilium*   (19. 7)
   *ad matris propinquae sinum festinus ut viderat convolavit*   (21. 3)

Consentius

> *ad neptis suae Asterii comitis filiae, potentissimae feminae*
> *auxilium convolaret* (*Ep.* 11\*. 4. 3)
> *ad sancti ac beatissimi Patrocli . . . auxilium convolarem*
> (23. 1)

The similarities between the narratives of Severus and Consentius are not confined, however, to diction and imagery. Despite sharp differences in personality, Severus and Consentius have surprisingly similar views on the position of orthodoxy and the necessity of religious coercion. For example, both the *Epistula Severi* and *Ep.* 11\* present Catholic orthodoxy as beleaguered in a world 'swarming' with Jews and heretics. Far from being dominant and aggressive, orthodoxy is weak and in need of a catalyst, a man of fiery zeal who will confront the formidable opponents arrayed against Catholicism. Both narratives make clear that religious error, whether in the form of Judaism or heresy, is firmly entrenched at the highest levels of secular power and impervious to verbal persuasion. Only the imposition of terror can hope to prevail against such resistance.

This pattern is readily apparent in Severus' narrative. We have already noted his emphasis on Minorca's isolation and the weakness of the Christians there (see above pp. 27–8). Catholicism is hardly triumphant, in his view, at least not on Minorca. Although Jamona is relatively safe from Jewish 'attacks', since Jews will not even accept hospitality there, Magona is 'seething' with so many Jews that 'Christ's church was being wounded by them daily' (3. 6). Yet the attitude of Magona's Christians is one of 'complacency' (4. 4, cf. 5. 1). A catalyst, in this case St Stephen, is necessary to disrupt the status quo and fire the faithful with a spirit of confrontation. Like other writers of anti-Jewish polemic, Severus employs all the conventional vocabulary of warfare to describe this confrontation with the Jews: *exercitus, certamen, proelium, bellum, contentio, pugna, indutiae.*[155] The fighting is fierce, even house to house: 'In every public place, battles were waged against the Jews over the Law, in every house struggles over the faith' (5. 2). But Magona's Christians are 'humble . . . in strength' (6. 4), deployed against a religious enemy of seemingly insuperable

---

[155] *Exercitus*: 6. 4; 8. 3; 9. 1; 27. 5; *certamen*: 6. 4; 8. 2–3; 12. 6; *proelium*: 5. 2; 8. 1; 27. 5; *bellum*: 7. 3; 9. 1; *contentio*: 12. 12; *pugna*: 5. 2; *indutiae*: 6. 4.

power. They gain a 'victory which no one dared hope for and which no one could expect' (8. 3). The unusual wealth of detail about Magona's Jewish notables further emphasizes the formidable power of the Jewish opposition. Not only do they control the town of Magona, but their power extends, through Count Litorius, all the way to the imperial court.

Verbal persuasion stands little chance in such conditions. Although Severus composed an anti-Jewish tract (*commoni-torium*) to assist him in debate, the events of the letter suggest that he put little faith in words alone. The Jews, for their part, clearly feared violence and were allegedly stockpiling weapons, 'desiring death even, in defence of their religion' (8. 4). When Severus appeared in Magona on 2 February and demanded a debate, they distrusted his motives and refused, initially at least, to be drawn out. When a debate finally did take place three days later on the site of the ruined synagogue, Severus' fears came true, since Theodorus debated 'boldly' concerning the Law, 'mocking and twisting' the bishop's points and making it plain to the Christian throng 'that he could not be vanquished by human arguments' (16. 3).

Only through divine intervention and the application of terror can the Jews be made to see truth. Having fired the Christians with 'zeal for the faith', Stephen withdraws to make way for Christ, whose 'power' (*virtus*) drives the Jews relentlessly on towards conversion. As Severus puts it, 'Christ, whose "kingdom dwells not in talk but in power" [1 Cor. 4: 20], achieved everything with his own forces and without us even uttering a word' (8. 3). The principal symbol of Christ's coercive power is the Lion of Judah, seen by Theodorus in a dream a month or two before the burning of the synagogue.[156] Theodorus, it will be recalled, dreamt that he was warned of a lion lurking within the synagogue, and, although frightened, he peered into the building only to see monks singing psalms (11. 2–6). The sight of the monks, however, instilled 'terror' in him, and if he had not raced to his kinswoman, who symbolizes the church, he could not have 'escaped the force of that deadly terror' (11. 5). The Lion returns at key moments in the

[156] Amengual i Batle, *Els orígens del cristianisme*, i. 82–9 suggests that Severus may have been inspired to use the image of the Lion by Gregory of Elvira. Cf. *Tractatus*, 13. 24–8 (*CCL* 69. 103–4).

narrative, on each occasion terrifying the reluctant Jews. On 2 February, when Severus arrived in Magona, they adamantly refused to meet at either the church or the synagogue until they were 'in the end driven by terror of that Lion' to gather at Severus' lodgings (12. 7). In the dramatic street scene when some of the Jews mistakenly believed that Theodorus had agreed to convert, Severus again invokes that 'terrible Lion', whose pursuit caused the frightened Jews to scatter in confusion. He notes further that Theodorus was standing on the very spot where he had been 'smitten with terror of the Lion' in his dream (16. 11).

'Now what tongue can speak forth,' asks Severus, 'the things which, by the power of Christ, befell those who fled into forests or caves?' (18. 1). The longest of these conversion narratives is the tale of Meletius and Innocentius, who had fled the public square when they believed Theodorus had agreed to convert and had taken refuge in the hills. While resting in a lonely spot in the hills, Meletius senses vaguely that he is the victim of daemonic possession. He confesses that the phrase 'Christ, in your name' implanted itself in his mind from the moment of his brother's conversion, and, although he knows it is blasphemous, he cannot rid himself of it. With the encouragement of Innocentius, he attempts to expel the hateful thought physically through his mouth or nose, but his shrieks and garbled cries, convulsions, and profanities are all in vain, for 'the fire of good health had penetrated to the depth of his marrow' (18. 10). Still unsubdued by Christ's power, he persuades Innocentius that they should hide out on a farm until the opportunity to emigrate presents itself. As they make their way through unknown country, however, they become lost and are reduced first to a state of 'anxiety' and then to such a state of 'fearful desperation' that they begin to invoke the dreaded name of Christ, and are led back to the town 'against their will and against their plan' (18. 23).

In speeches whose contents are scrupulously authenticated by Severus (cf. 16. 13–16; 18. 3–20; 19. 1–10), the Jews themselves discuss with brutal frankness the motives compelling them to accept conversion, 'For there was almost no one who did not testify that he had openly felt the power of Christ' (19. 2). Reuben, for example, appeals to Theodorus' basic desire to maintain both his physical safety and his political prominence:

What do you fear, Lord Theodorus? If you truly wish to be safe and honoured and wealthy, believe in Christ, just as I too have believed. Right now you are standing, and I am seated with bishops; if you should believe, you will be seated, and I will be standing before you.   (16. 14–15)

Meletius, younger brother of Theodorus, sees exile as the only possible alternative after his brother's apostasy, 'since hatred against our religion has increased to such an extent among all people on this island that whoever does not abandon his fatherland will be unable to retain his fathers' faith' (18. 19). He urges Innocentius that they accept a 'voluntary exile' since the 'hatred of the citizens' will drive them to it even if they are unwilling (18. 19). The 'voluntary' character of this exile is made clear by the abortive flight of Innocentius' sister-in-law, who took ship as soon as she heard of his conversion. As Severus concedes, 'We not only permitted her to do this, we even encouraged her, because she could not be turned to faith in Christ by either words or miracles' (26. 2). This clarifies too Innocentius' near desperation at his wife's obstinate refusal to convert for nearly four days after his own capitulation (27. 1–7). All of the Jews are being given a choice between conversion and exile, perhaps even death. No speech conveys more dramatically the atmosphere of intimidation, however, than that of Galilaeus to the assembled synagogue. Like everyone else, Galilaeus, a young kinsman of Theodorus, is stunned at the burning of the synagogue and terrified by the threat of Christian violence. Fear verging on panic drives him, though a youth, to flout convention by speaking out in a public meeting:

I call you all to witness that I cannot be a Jew. For on my estate I have Christian partners by whose hatred I may be killed if I wish to persevere in Judaism. Therefore, I will heed the danger to my life and will set out right now for the church to escape the death being prepared for me.   (19. 4–5)

The eminent Caecilianus quickly cuts him off, and although he is not 'all aflutter' like the young Galilaeus, he none the less concedes that Galilaeus' fears are well-founded and that he himself shares them. He goes on to argue that they must all abandon the 'mockery of this religion' which they lack the strength to defend (19. 9). Caecilianus and his brother Florianus, who are both Fathers of the Jews, lead the revolt which splits the synagogue as some Jews go immediately to the church.

Many of the themes just outlined can be found as well in Consentius' *Ep.* 11\*, written in 419 (perhaps 420) as a rebuke of Augustine's 'soft' treatment of Donatists in North Africa. Spaniards favouring a 'soft' response to Priscillianists are pointing to the North African model and to the personal authority of Augustine himself. Consentius' view, however, seems to be that coercion should be applied wherever it will work, as it will, in his opinion, in Spain. Hence, a 'hard' line is in order and he hopes that the orthodox bishops in Gaul will appeal to the Emperor Honorius:

Perhaps inflamed by the fire of a greater zeal, just as is certainly true in my case, they will bring these matters to the attention of a great prince. They will work hard to ensure that this cancerous teaching which has secretly expanded by gradual stages through the whole world will be cauterized throughout all the provinces in a general ruling.[157]

But the similarity of outlook between Consentius and Severus emerges also from the basic narrative pattern in *Ep.* 11\*'s account of Fronto's undercover operation against Priscillianists in Tarragona.

Without a lengthy exposition, it is impossible to do justice to the baroque twists and turns of this bizarre narrative, its dramatic confrontations, and the melodramatic atmosphere of terror and intimidation.[158] Augustine, for his part, was clearly shocked and composed the treatise *Contra Mendacium* (we now

---

[157] *Ep.* 11\*. 24. 3: *maioris, sicut apud me certum est, zeli igne succensi fortasse haec etiam ad aures incliti principis referentes elaborabunt ut, quoniam per universum iam orbem huius dogmatis cancer occulte serpendo protentus est, per omnes provincias uniformis sententiae cauteribus amburatur.*

[158] Consentius assures Augustine that he is relating faithfully what Fronto told him, but this does not imply verbatim accuracy (cf. 11\*. 1. 6, 24. 1). I assume that the rhetorical dress and 'colouring' of the account are due to Consentius, not Fronto. I cite *Ep.* 11\* with the chapter and section numbers from the edition of J. Divjak (ed.), *Sancti Aureli Augustini epistolae ex duobus codicibus nuper in lucem prolatae*, *CSEL* 88 (Vienna, 1981).

realize) in response to Consentius' unscrupulous tactics in his campaign against heresy. Modern scholars have been understandably intrigued but perplexed by the account. It has been suggested that *Ep.* 11* is a 'hagiographical pastiche', but I doubt that we are dealing with a conscious pastiche of a hagiographical text.[159] Like the *Epistula Severi*, *Ep.* 11* presents a beleaguered orthodoxy in a world swarming with the unorthodox and suggests that terror is the only response that has a hope of securing victory for the orthodox party.

Just as Magona 'seethed' with Jews, so the Spanish mainland, in Consentius' account, 'swarmed' with so many Priscillianists at this time (*c.* 418–19) that the 'barbarians seemed trivial in comparison' (1. 4).[160] Just as Minorca needed the catalyst of Stephen's arrival to ignite the local Christians, a solitary monk, Fronto, a man in whom the 'Holy Spirit kindles the most ardent flames of zeal for the faith', emerges as the representative of orthodoxy to undertake the campaign against Spanish heretics.[161] Severus had consistently emphasized the humility and weakness of Minorca's Christians. Similarly, Consentius stresses the isolation and weakness of the proponent of orthodox Catholicism. Fronto is alone and of humble rank, branded by his opponents as a man 'poor in goods, rich in lies, armed only with boldness, and destitute of innocence' (5. 1). He confesses himself to be a 'poor man' (8. 2) ranged against powerful forces, and he regards himself a mere 'dead flea' (7. 3). Like Severus, Consentius carefully notes the high social rank, wealth, and learning of the religious enemy. Fronto's opponents, all allegedly dabblers in heresy and magic, are invariably people of high rank, like the priest in Tarragona called Severus, a 'leader of this sect noted for his wealth and power, and also famous for his literary ability' (2. 3), Bishop Sagittius of Lérida, a man 'skilled in law and learned in literature' (16. 3), and Syagrius of Huesca, a 'wealthy man' (17. 5).

[159] Moreau, 'Lecture de la Lettre 11* de Consentius à Augustin', 215–23, who argues that the letter contains a number of features common in hagiographical works, particularly accounts of the early martyrs: a lone, pious Christian bravely opposing a phalanx of unbelievers; the presence of a high-ranking official with whom the martyr frequently discusses the faith; a clichéd psychological presentation of the two sides; the presence of miracles.

[160] On Priscillian, see H. Chadwick, *Priscillian of Avila* (Oxford, 1976).

[161] *Ep.* 11* 1. 2: *verum accidit, ut quidam famulus Christi nomine Fronto cui spiritus sanctus flagrantissimas fidelis zeli suggerit flammas subitus adveniret.*

Once threatened with accusations of heresy, the entrenched power of the religious enemy becomes both conspicuous and effective, as it was on Minorca as well. Severus quickly marshals his kinsmen and friends, 'very powerful people' (7. 2). We learn that he is related by marriage (*affinis*) to Asterius, the *comes Hispaniarum*, the highest-ranking Roman officer in Spain at the time. Called the 'first man in the Count's household' (21. 3), Severus takes refuge in the Count's palace and places a kinswoman under the protection of Asterius' daughter, who is referred to as Severus' 'niece' (*neptis*) and a 'very powerful woman' in her own right (4. 3). He is able to portray the accusation against him as a slanderous attack on the 'Count himself, his household, and his daughter' (7. 2). The bishops mentioned invariably brand Fronto a 'deceitful and lying accuser' (9. 2), even threatening him with death (11. 1). The heretics deny everything and succeed in suppressing the truth until one of the bishops, frightened by a dream, exposes the cover-up. Still the community holds firm against Fronto. The bishops burn the minutes of the tribunal, restore everyone to communion, and drive Fronto out of Tarragona.

As in the *Epistula Severi*, terror pervades Consentius' narrative. There is no possibility of dialogue with these heretics, since they refuse even to acknowledge their heresy. Consentius and Fronto did not realize apparently the extreme danger Fronto would encounter after he had 'launched hostilities'. He refuses to go to the Count's palace (8. 3), and for good reason, since one of the daughter's servants eventually does try to kill him (13. 1). He repeatedly stresses the 'hatred' he stirred up among the people and he concedes that he did not dare to leave the church (12. 6). The proponent of orthodoxy possesses truth, but is crushed by the superior forces of heresy (8. 1; 21. 1). Christ, 'who knows all secrets and settles all cases' (2. 4), must appear in power to assist the weak orthodox party and to terrify the heretics in turn.[162]

---

[162] Christ's power is present to Fronto's weakness, so that even the Count is 'terrified' (8. 1); Christ helps Fronto to reply boldly to the Count (8. 3); Bishop Agapius' fury is suppressed by the 'power of Christ' (11. 2); Christ the 'judge' (*vindex*) strikes down the servant who attempted to kill Fronto (13. 3); Bishop Syagrius decides to tell the truth after being 'terrified by a miraculous vision of . . . Christ' (15.3); Bishop Sagittius, 'terrified by fear', is forced to restore parts of a codex that he had allegedly excised (20. 4).

In sum, the similarities between the accounts of events on Minorca and in Tarragona raise the possibility that Consentius was more deeply involved in the composition of the *Epistula Severi* than we had suspected. Josep Amengual i Batle has suggested that Consentius was the 'father' of the *Epistula Severi* and has expressed the suspicion that he was in fact the moving force behind events in Magona in February 418.[163] These hypotheses may be correct, but it should be noted that Consentius states quite clearly that he took no part in events in Magona and that Severus intended to write the account himself (*Ep.* 12\*. 13. 6: *irrupit propositum meum summis viribus caritatis et, ut epistolam quae rei gestae ordinem contineret ipse conscriberet, sola a me verba mutuatus est*). Severus took the initiative in approaching Consentius, presumably because he thought he could benefit from the latter's superior literary culture. He was apparently willing to be guided not only in the choice of diction and imagery, but in the whole shape he gave to the narrative. The features of the *Epistula Severi* that make it so valuable a narrative for the historian, its wealth of detail about the Jews of Magona and the frank portrayal of religious coercion, appear to be due to the counsel of Consentius.

## VIII. CONVERSION AND ITS AFTERMATH

It is difficult to discern from the narrative what Severus understood by the idea of 'conversion' or even what precisely he did to 'convert' the Jews.[164] Twice in the letter he mentions making the sign of the cross on the foreheads of new converts, which was conventional at the beginning of the catechumenate, as was the practice of noting down their names in a register (20. 3).[165] Under normal circumstances, catechumens would at

---

[163] Amengual i Batle, *Els orígens del cristianisme*, i. 215.

[164] Severus appears untroubled by the problem of forced, and therefore feigned, conversion. For the more nuanced views of Augustine, see P. R. L. Brown, 'St. Augustine's Attitude to Religious Coercion', in *Religion and Society in the Age of Saint Augustine* (London, 1977), 260–78.

[165] Cf. 15. 3: *Ruben ... signum salutare suscepit*; 17. 2–3: *deprecabantur ut Christi characterem a me ... susciperent ... ilico in frontibus eorum signum salutis impressimus*. On 'becoming a Christian' from the catechumenate up to Easter week, see F. van der Meer, *Augustine the Bishop* (London, 1961), 353–87.

their own discretion have their names noted down for baptism, at which point they would be considered *competentes*, and, during the final few weeks before Easter, they would prepare for the great event with fasts, vigils, exorcisms, and final instructions.[166] In the drama of forced conversions, however, normal conventions might well be ignored, since bishops needed to do everything possible to prevent backsliding.[167] When Theodorus leads his flock to the church, Severus speaks of an old man who 'presented to us his limbs, by now feeble with decay, that he might be renewed through baptism as quickly as possible'.[168] Moreover, he claims at 29. 1: 'Although the eight days in which these events occurred were before the beginning of Lent, they were celebrated by us as if it were Easter.' This clearly alludes to the conventional practice of baptism at the Paschal vigil and implies that, in the present instance, Minorca's Jews were catechumens for only a few hours or a few days before being baptized willy-nilly.[169] Furthermore, the Jewish leaders have been compelled to accept responsibility for providing both the funds and the labourers for the construction of a new church on the site of the ruined synagogue (30. 2).

Conversion did not lead to loss of civic influence for Magona's prominent Jews. In a number of passages in the letter, Severus alludes to the immediate present and the situation of the Jewish notables. Of the seven instances when Severus uses the phrase 'even now' or 'still today' (*etiam nunc*), four or perhaps five seem genuinely to describe conditions at the time when he was composing the letter in March–April 418.[170] Theodorus had been particularly concerned to maintain his pre-eminent position among the Jews, agreeing to convert, but parleying for more time so that, in his own words, 'I may

---

[166] Cf. *Itinerarium Egeriae* 45. 1 (*CSEL* 39. 96): *Nam qui dat nomen suum, ante diem quadragesimarum dat et omnium nomina annotat presbyter [. . .] et sic adducuntur unus et unus conpetens*.

[167] Blumenkranz, *Juifs et chrétiens*, 148–52.

[168] *Ep. Sev.* 22: *nobisque putrefacta iam senio membra ut quantocius per baptismum regenerarentur ingessit*.

[169] Easter baptism was preferable, but not strictly necessary, cf. Aug. *Serm.* 210. 2 (*PL* 38. 1048): *cum per totum annum, sicut unicuique vel necessitas fuerit vel voluntas, non prohibeatur a baptismo*.

[170] Two passages with *etiam nunc* clearly refer to past time, cf. 16. 19; 18. 24. Other passages clearly refer to present time, that is, the time of composition, cf. 3. 1; 18. 4; 20. 12.

reap a greater reward for my conversion by the conversion of the others as well' (16. 16). He apparently achieved his goal, since Severus claims that Theodorus 'even now is held to be the *patronus* of his fellow citizens', and Caecilianus is described as a 'worthy man, and so eminent not only among the Jews but also in the city that even now he has been elected *defensor*'.[171] Even more intriguing is a comment made by Consentius in *Ep.* 12* where he describes his consultation with Severus about the proposal to write an account of the miraculous conversion. Immediately following his mention of Severus' project and the breakdown of his own resolution not to write anything, he continues:

Thereafter, a greater desire grew in me to transgress the resolution (*legis*) that I had prescribed for myself, and I resolved (that my sluggish memory might be assisted by my reading of Scripture, which, albeit lazy and negligent, was none the less fresh) to produce for our leader some arms against the Jews by whom we were hard pressed in battle (*aliqua adversus Iudaeos quorum proeliis urgebamur duci nostro arma producerem*), but with this rule (*lege*), that my name not be mentioned in the task. (*Ep.* 12*. 13. 7)

Consentius composed this passage in 419, perhaps a year after the conversion in February 418, and he is describing the period following his literary encounter with Severus, which took place after 9 February and before Severus completed his narrative in March–April. But who is 'our leader' hard pressed in battles with Jews and in need of arms? It has been assumed that the *dux* must be Asterius, the *comes Hispaniarum*, but the military language is metaphorical, not literal.[172] The leaders of the campaign against the Jews were Catholic bishops, not army generals. The bishop under discussion in the passage is Severus himself, the leader of the campaign against the Jews of Magona. Consentius had already broken his resolution not to take up his pen when he assisted Severus with the *Epistula*, but now an even greater desire to break his resolution has grown in

---

[171] 6. 3: *etiam nunc patronus municipum habetur*; 19. 6: *vir honestus, et non solum inter Iudaeos verum etiam in civitate usque adeo praecipuus, ut etiam nunc defensor civitatis electus sit.*

[172] Wankenne in Divjak, *Œuvres de Saint Augustin*, 492–3 assumes that the *dux* must be Asterius.

him, and so he has resolved to produce an anti-Jewish tract
(*arma*) for his leader, but with a new rule or resolution (*lege*) not
put his own name to the work. An important conclusion
follows from the mention of this tract *adversus Iudaeos*.[173] Consentius composed the tract after the conversion of early February, which suggests that Severus continued to be hard pressed
in debates with Jewish leaders in the weeks and months after
the events of early February. The miraculous conversion, it
appears, was less successful than Severus would have us
believe.

## IX. THE TEXT AND EDITIONS OF THE *EPISTULA SEVERI*[174]

The *Epistula Severi* was first published by Cardinal Baronius in
*Annales Ecclesiastici* in 1594. Baronius informs us that he had
found in the Vatican collection a copy of Severus' letter whole
and undamaged in any way, and that his text derives from that
manuscript.[175] Two manuscripts currently in the Vatican
Library contain the *Epistula Severi*: *Codex Palatinus-Latinus 856*
and *Codex Latinus 1188*. Since the Palatine manuscript was not
acquired by the Vatican until 1623, Baronius' edition was
apparently copied from *Codex Latinus 1188*. In the manuscript
tradition, the *Epistula Severi* generally appears with a group of
works describing the discovery and translation of Stephen's
relics. They were first published in Louvain at the end of the
sixteenth century as an appendix to an edition of the collected
works of Augustine. In 1648 the Maurist Fathers in Paris
published their great edition of Augustine's works, in which
they included, as an appendix to the *City of God*, the various

---

[173] Amengual i Batle, *Els orígens del cristianisme*, i. 214 suspects that Consentius' tract
*Adversus Iudaeos* is the *commonitorium* attached by Severus to the *Ep. Sev.* (8. 1–2), but
note that the *commonitorium* was composed before (*qualia praeparaverimus arma*) the conversion of February 418, whereas the tract *Adversus Iudaeos* was clearly composed after
the conversion (*Ep.* 12*. 13. 7). On the other hand, the tract *Adversus Iudaeos* could be
the 'twelve chapters against the Jews' mentioned at 12*. 15. 2.

[174] On the history of the text and its editions, see Seguí Vidal, *La carta-encíclica*, 15–
29; Amengual i Batle, *Els orígens del cristianisme*, i. 63–4.

[175] *Annales Ecclesiastici*, v (Rome, 1594), 419: *Datum est . . . nobis eiusdem protomartyris
gratia ut inter scribendas Vaticanae Bibliothecae antiquitates eamdem reperiremus Severi epistolam
integram in nullo detrimentum passam.*

works concerning Stephen's relics, including the *Epistula Severi*. They reprinted Baronius' *editio princeps*, but introduced variant readings without clarifying whether they had consulted new manuscripts or were simply emending the text as they had found it in Baronius. In 1787, a Minorcan priest, Father Roig, published a text based on that of Baronius with emendations based on a comparison of *Codex Latinus 1188* and *Codex Palatinus-Latinus 856*.[176]

From the point of view of modern scholars, the most important publication of Severus' letter was obviously that of Migne, who included the work in two different volumes of the *Patrologia Latina*. In 1841–2, Migne re-published the Maurist edition of Augustine in a twelve-volume collection, which was later inserted into the *Patrologia* series as volumes 32 to 47. He reproduced the Maurist text of the *Epistula Severi*, which, it will be recalled, was Baronius' text with some emendations of indeterminate origin, and that version appeared in *PL* 41. 821–32. In *PL* 20, published in 1845, he reproduced Baronius' text exactly as he found it in the *Annales Ecclesiastici*, published in 1594. Thus, all editions of the *Epistula Severi* published before 1937 derived from the *editio princeps* of Baronius, which was itself based on the transcription of a single manuscript in the Vatican Library.

In a thesis published in 1937, G. Seguí Vidal attempted the first critical edition of the *Epistula Severi*.[177] Seguí Vidal discovered, on comparing *Codex Latinus 1188* with Baronius' text and its descendants, that there were numerous discrepancies, too numerous, he reasoned, to be the result of careless copying. He concluded that Baronius' text must have derived from some other manuscript whose existence had escaped his notice. A long and fruitless search in the Vatican's catalogues led him, however, to the conclusion that there was no 'lost' manuscript. The discrepancies between Baronius' text and *Codex Latinus 1188* had to be attributed, in his view, to Baronius' copyist, who had transcribed the text so carelessly that all published editions of the *Epistula Severi* were riddled

[176] Mn. Antoni Roig i Rexart, *De Sacris apud minorem Balearem antistibus, Severo potissimum deque istius Epistola exercitatio et in eamdem Epistolam animadversiones* (Palma, 1787), 101–36.

[177] Seguí Vidal, *La carta-encíclica*.

with errors, since all published editions derived from Baronius. Since the publication of Seguí Vidal's monograph, scholars in Spain have continued to show an interest in the text of *Epistula Severi*.[178] We should note in particular the work of J. Amengual i Batle, who has published (in Catalan) a critical edition of the *Epistula Severi* with facing translation as well as several articles on related topics and a history of Christianity in the Balearic Islands in which the *Epistula* figures prominently. Amengual i Batle first published his critical edition in an appendix to *Els orígens del cristianisme a les Balears i el seu desenvolupament fins a l'època musulmana* in 1985.[179] He discovered two manuscripts unknown to Seguí Vidal and produced a new text with many improvements on previous editions, followed by a translation into Catalan. The text and translation were reprinted in *Correspondència amb Sant Agustí*, Vol. I, which included editions and translations of the letters of Consentius and Severus' epistle.[180]

The *Epistula Severi* is preserved in nine manuscripts, of which only seven are useful in the compilation of the text, since two versions are demonstrably copies of other extant manuscripts:

**P** *Palatinus-Latinus 856*. Tenth-century codex copied at Lorsch and acquired by the Vatican Library from the *Biblioteca del Conte Palatino* in 1623; twenty-four folios. The manuscript contains only the *Epistula Severi* ($1^v$–$15^v$) and part of the *De Miraculis Sancti Stephani*: book 1 entire ($16^r$–$23^v$) and book 2, chapter 3 ($23^v$–$24^r$). Script in a single column by one hand from the second half of the tenth century, with the exception of folio $1^r$, the title page, where we find *Severus episcopus de revelatione quadam sibi facta in altare* in a different hand.

**W** *Wolfenbüttel 2738* (= *Guelferbytanus 76.14 Aug. fol.*) Twelfth-century codex in double columns containing hagiographical works, including the *De Miraculis Sancti Stephani* and the *Epistula Severi* ($29^v$–$31^v$).

---

[178] E. Lafuente Hernandez, *Epistola Severi episcopi. Edición paleográfica y transcripción latina seguidas de las versiones castellana y catalan de su texto* (Minorca, 1981). This publication consists of a photographic reproduction of *Codex Vaticanus Latinus 1188* with a facing Latin transcription followed by translations into Spanish and Catalan.

[179] The text is printed in vol. 2, pp. 12–65. In addition to many other improvements to the text, Amengual provided it with its first serviceable system of chapter and section numbers, which I have adopted in the interest of uniformity.

[180] J. Amengual i Batle (ed.), *Correspondència amb Sant Agustí*, i (Barcelona, 1987), 38–84.

**V** *Vaticanus Latinus 1188*. Fifteenth-century codex in double columns containing fifty-three works, mostly saints' lives and passions; five works concern St Stephen: the *Epistula Aviti* (82$^v$), the *Epistula Luciani* (82$^v$–84$^v$), the translation of Stephen's body to Constantinople (84$^v$–86$^r$), the *Epistula Severi* (86$^r$–91$^v$), and the *De Miraculis Sancti Stephani* (91$^v$–100$^v$).

**S** *Saint Sépulcre 846*. Eleventh-century codex copied at the monastery of Saint Sépulcre near Cambrai and currently owned by the Bibliothèque Municipale de Cambrai (number 846); 144 folios in a single column containing lives of saints and churchmen as well as martyr accounts and a group of works on St Stephen, including the *De Miraculis Sancti Stephani* (75$^r$-99$^v$), the *Epistula Severi* (99$^v$–111$^r$), and an account of Stephen's translation to Constantinople (111$^r$–114$^v$).

**A** *Saint Aubert 856*. Thirteenth-century codex copied at the monastery of Saint Aubert near Cambrai and now, like *Saint Sépulcre 846*, kept in the Bibliothèque Municipale de Cambrai (number 856). It contains many martyr accounts and a group of works on St Stephen: the *Epistula Luciani* (27$^v$–31$^r$), an account of his translation to Constantinople (33$^v$–36$^v$), the *De Miraculis Sancti Stephani* (36$^v$–54$^r$), and the *Epistula Severi* (54$^v$–62$^v$).

**G** *Saint Ghislain 3286*. Eleventh-century codex deriving from the monastery of Saint Ghislain and now owned by the Bibliothèque Royale de Belgique (no. II, 973, formally Phillips 364); 130 folios in an eleventh-century hand. On folio 1, we find *Liber Sancti Gilleni*, on folio 122$^v$ *Liber Sancti Gysleni*. Seventeen of twenty-nine texts in the manuscript concern the relics of St Stephen.

**C** *Charleville 117*. Twelfth-century codex copied at Signy and now owned by the Bibliothèque Municipale de Charleville (number 117); 164 folios containing mostly works on the life and miracles of St Martin and two works concern Stephen: the *Epistula Luciani* (140$^r$–146$^v$) and the *Epistula Severi* (147$^r$-163$^v$).

Two other manuscripts contain the *Epistula Severi*, but are demonstrably copies of *Codex Latinus 1188*. The first is a sixteenth-century manuscript in the Biblioteca Valliceliana in Rome (*Codex C. 16*), containing a miscellany of works, including the *Epistula Severi* (124$^v$–135$^r$). A note on folio 124 refers to a manuscript in the Vatican collection: *Habetur in Biblioteca Vaticana a sinistris num. 234. Liber inscribitur: Passiones sanctorum pagina 86*. The note alludes to *Codex Latinus 1188*, the only manuscript containing the *Epistula Severi* in the Vatican in the sixteenth century.[181] Finally, a seventeenth-century manuscript in the Bibliothèque Nationale in Paris (*Parisienis Latinus 12327*) contains the *Epistula Severi* (19ʳ–32ʳ), but a note indicates that the text was copied from the manuscript in the Biblioteca Valliceliana: *Ms. Bibliothecae Vallicelii c. 16, f. 124*.[182]

Thus, seven of the nine surviving manuscripts of the *Epistula Severi* are of use in establishing the text and can be divided into three families with the following affiliation:

Severus

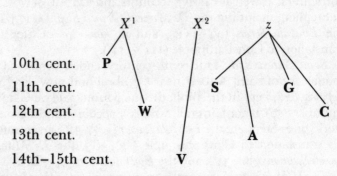

| | |
|---|---|
| 10th cent. | P |
| 11th cent. | S G |
| 12th cent. | W C |
| 13th cent. | A |
| 14th–15th cent. | V |

The extant manuscripts bear witness to three separate traditions deriving from Severus' original text. The first is represented by **P** and **W**, the second by the sole witness of **V**, and the third by the group of four manuscripts **S**, **A**, **G**, and **C**. I have attached particular weight to the readings of **P** and **W**, especially **P**, which is both the oldest and the most reliable of the extant manuscripts. **P** and **W** frequently preserve correct readings which have been corrupted in all other manuscripts. The second tradition is represented by **V**, which, although a late manuscript, is an important witness and a useful control on the readings of **P** and **W**. The third family is represented by four manuscripts (**SAGC**), whose common archetype I have called *z*. When three members of this third family concur in their

---

[181] A. Poncelet, *Catalogus codicum hagiographicorum Latinorum Bibliothecarum Romanarum praeter quam Vaticanae* (Subsidia Hagiographica 9; Brussels, 1909), 385, Codex C. 16. Poncelet notes: *Exscripta ex codice Vaticano 'plut. sinistr. 4, num. 234, pag. 86', id est ex hodierno codice Vaticano lat. 1188, fol. 86–91ᵛ.*

[182] Seguí Vidal, *La carta-encíclica*, 23–4 claims that his inspection of these manuscripts confirms that they are copies of *Cod. Lat. 1188*.

reading and the fourth member's variant is easily explained, I have reported the majority reading as $z$. **S** and **A**, however, clearly derive from a common intermediary source, since they frequently err together in reporting a variant not found in **G** and **C** or in any other manuscript. In some cases I have considered the agreement of **G** and **C** as, in effect, a majority reading, and have reported it as the reading of the archetype $z$. My goal has been to report accurately and thoroughly the readings of all three manuscript traditions, noting those variants that can be of use in the reconstruction of Severus' text. In instances when corrections are found in the manuscripts, the original and corrected reading are reported with superscript numbers, e.g. $P^1$ and $P^2$. In the interest of economy, I have preferred conventional classical spelling and have chosen not to report the manuscripts' numerous orthographical variations, except in the few cases where those variations are essential for establishing the text. Similarly, I have not reported the frequent variations in word order. In most instances, two of the three families of manuscripts have agreed on this point and I have usually preferred the majority reading.

# EPISTULA SEVERI


# THE LETTER OF SEVERUS

Sanctissimis ac beatissimis dominis episcopis, presbyteris, diaconibus et universae fraternitati totius orbis terrarum, Severus episcopus misericordia Dei indigens et omnium ultimus in Christo Redemptore nostro aeternam salutem.

5 1. Cum 'opera Dei revelare et confiteri honorificum esse' Raphael archangelus moneat, profecto silere vel celare miracula Christi periculosum est. In quibus tamen annuntiandis maior gratia est si communi ac simplici sermone referantur. (2) Celatur enim quodammodo speciosissima pulchritudo virtutis, 10 si abundantiori eloquio circumlita fuerit ac fucata. Quapropter ego quoque magnalia, quae apud nos Christus operatus est, Beatitudini vestrae non compto sed veridico sermone referre aggrediar.

2. Insula Minorica una ex Balearibus insulis est, quarum 15 nomen cunctis populis saecularium quoque auctorum litteris pervulgatum est. (2) Haec, inter Mauritaniam Caesariensem et Hispaniam medio propemodum aequoris spatio sita, angustis admodum terminis clauditur, (3) longitudine triginta latitudine vero decem ferme milia passuum habens. (4) Quae nunc 20 idcirco commemoravi, ut agnosci possit 'contemptibilia mundi' a Domino non solum in hominibus sed etiam in locis eligi. (5) In hac itaque insula, quae omnium terrarum parvitate, ariditate, asperitate postrema est, duo parva oppida a Poenis, sicut inditum nomen indicio est, e regione fundata 25 sunt: Iamona ad occasum, Magona ad orientem spectat. (6) In his mihi omnium mortalium ultimo nuper sacerdotalis officii pondus impositum est.

3. Sed Iamona antiquum a Deo munus etiam nunc retinet, ut

1–2 Item Severi de miraculis sancti Stephani protomartyris in Iudaeorum conversione apud se patratis *add.* W      Incipit epistola Severi episcopi de laude et de miraculis sancti Stephani protomartyris *add.* V      (Incipit) epistola Severi episcopi de conversione Iudaeorum apud Minoricam insulam meritis sancti Stephani facta *add.* SA Prologus Severi episcopi in miraculis beati Stephani *add.* G      2 fraternitati *WVz*: fraternitatis P      3 Dei *om.* PW      4 domino *post* Christo *add.* W 5 opera *WVz*: operam P      Dei *om.* W      6 archangelus *PVz*: angelus W 6–7 vel celare *om.* W      miracula *PWz*: opera V      7 tamen *om.* Vz      annuntiandis *PVz*: nuntiandis W      10 (h)abundantiori *PW*: (h)abundantiore Vz circumlita fuerit ac fucata *Vz*: circumligata fuerit ac fuscata PW      12 compto *PWz*: computo V      14 Descriptio Minoricae *ante* insula *add.* V      insulis *om.* W

80

To the most Holy and Blessed Lord Bishops, Presbyters, Deacons and to the Universal Brotherhood of the whole world, Bishop Severus, needful of God's mercy and most unworthy of all men, sends an eternal blessing in Christ our Redeemer.

1. Just as the Archangel Raphael warns that it is honourable to acknowledge and reveal the works of God [Tobit 12: 20], surely it is dangerous to veil in silence or conceal the miracles of Christ. Their proclamation produces greater pleasure, however, if they are recounted in familiar and unadorned language, (2) for the radiant beauty of virtue is somehow obscured if she is rouged and painted with excessive eloquence. Wherefore, it will be with language that is not polished but truthful, that I shall undertake to recount for your Blessedness the miraculous deeds that Christ has performed among us.

2. Minorca is one of the Balearic Islands, whose name has been spread abroad among all peoples, even in the works of pagan writers. (2) It is located in the open sea almost midway between Mauretania and Spain and is confined within rather narrow boundaries, (3) being thirty miles long and ten miles wide. (4) I have mentioned these facts that it may be recognized how the 'lowly things of this world' [1 Cor. 1: 28] are chosen by the Lord not only in the case of people, but places as well. (5) On this island, the most forsaken of all lands due to its tiny size, dryness, and harshness, two small towns were founded opposite one another by the Carthaginians, as is indicated by the names given them: Jamona looks towards the west, Magona towards the east. (6) In these towns, the burden of episcopal office had recently been placed on me, most unworthy of all mortal men.

3. But Jamona retains even now an ancient favour from God,

quarum *PWz*: quorum *V*      16 Mauritaniam *PWVG*: Maritaniam *S*: maritimam *A*: Maurituniam *C*      17 Hispaniam: *WVz*: Spaniam *P*      medio *PVz*: medium *W*      18–19 longitudine ... latitudine *PWC*: longitudinem ... latitudinem *VSAG*      19 decem *om. V*      ferme *PW*²: fere *W*¹*Vz*      milia *om. W*      quae *PVz*: quam *W*      20 commemoravi *PWVGC*: memoravi *SA*      21 a *om. W*      23–4 a P(o)enis *PWz*: ophenis *V*      24 indicio *PWz*: indictio *V*¹, indictione *V*²      25 sunt *PWVG*: est *SAC*      Iamona *PWz*: Iammona *V*      28 nunc *om. W*

Iudaei habitare in ea nequaquam possint. (2) Multos siquidem id temere audentes, aut aegritudine praeventos ac repulsos aut morte subita extinctos aut etiam fulmine trucidatos tradit vetustas, adeo ut celebris huius rei fama ipsis quoque Iudaeis,
5 ne id ultra temptare audeant, metum fecerit. (3) Nec hoc fide indignum ducimus, cum etiam vulpes luposque et omnia noxia animalia deesse videamus, cum earum quae ad vescendum bonae sunt ferarum magna copia sit. (4) Illud etiam magis mirum est, quod colubri atque scorpiones sunt quidem
10 plurimi, sed amiserunt omnem nocendi violentiam. (5) Cum igitur Iamonam nullus Iudaeorum, qui lupis ac vulpibus feritate atque nequitia merito comparantur, ne hospitii quidem iure succedere audeat, (6) Magona tantis Iudaeorum populis velut colubris scorpionibusque fervebat, ut quotidie ab his
15 Christi ecclesia morderetur. (7) Sed antiquum illud carnale beneficium, nuper nobis spiritualiter renovatum est, ut illa, sicut scriptum est, 'generatio viperarum' quae venenatis ictibus saeviebat, subito divina virtute compulsa mortiferum illud virus incredulitatis abiecerit.
20 4. Namque diebus paene isdem, quibus ego tanti sacerdotii nomen, licet indignus, adeptus sum, presbyter quidam sancti- tate praecipuus ab Hierosolyma veniens, Magonae non longo tempore immoratus est. Qui postquam transvehi ad Hispanias, sicut desiderabat, nequivit, remeare denuo ad Africam statuit.
25 (2) Hic beati martyris Stephani reliquias, quae nuper revelatae sunt, cum ad Hispanias portare constituisset, ipso sine dubio martyre inspirante, in memorati oppidi ecclesia collocavit. (3) Quo facto, protinus ille, quem Dominus 'venit mittere in terram' et quem valde ardere cupit, caritatis eius ignis accensus
30 est. (4) Statim siquidem tepor noster incaluit et factum est cor nostrum, sicut scriptum est, 'ardens in via'. Nunc enim iam

---

1 Iudaei *PVz*: Iudaea *W*    2 ac *WSG*: et *P*: aut *VAC*    3 subita *PWz*: subitanea *V*    etiam *Vz*: iam *W, om. P*    7 etiam *post* quae *add. W*
8 bonae *PVz*: bona *W*    9–10 quidem plurimi *Pz*: plurimi *W*: quamplurimi *V*
11 Iamonam *PW*: Iamona *Vz*    ac vulpibus *Vz*: atque vulpibus *P*: vulpibusque *W*
12 nequitia *WVz*: nequitiae *P*    comparantur *PVz*: comparatur *W*    hospitii *PVz*: hospitis *W*    14 ut tradebatur *post* scorpionibusque *add. V*    16 spiritu- aliter renovatum *Wz*: in spirituale conversum *P*: spiritale renovatum *V*    18 sae- viebat *PVz*: serviebat *W*    24 nequivit *PWz*: requievit *V*    25 revelatae *WVz*: revelata *P*    26 portare *PVz*: deportare *W*    ipso *PWz*: ipsas *V*

namely that Jews are absolutely unable to live there. (2) Ancient tradition hands down that many Jews, if they rashly dared to try, were prevented by sickness and driven out, or laid low by sudden death, or even struck down by a thunderbolt. The tale is so well known that it has made the Jews themselves afraid, so that they no longer dare to attempt it. (3) Nor do we consider this fact unworthy of our faith, that we observe, on the one hand, an absence of wolves, foxes, and all harmful animals, while, on the other hand, there is a great abundance of those wild animals that are good to eat. (4) What is even more marvellous is that vipers and scorpions are indeed very plentiful, but have lost all ability to do violent harm.[1] (5) Although none of the Jews, who are rightly compared with wolves and foxes for fierceness and villainy, dares to approach Jamona, not even for the right of hospitality, (6) Magona seethed with so great a multitude of Jews, as if with vipers and scorpions, that Christ's church was being wounded by them daily.[2] (7) But that ancient, earthly favour was recently renewed for us in a spiritual sense, so that, as it is written, that generation of vipers [Luke 3: 7], which used to attack with venomous stings, suddenly under the compulsion of divine power has cast aside the lethal poison of unbelief.

4. At about that same period when I, although unworthy, assumed the title of episcopal office, a certain priest, conspicuous for his sanctity, came from Jerusalem and sojourned for a brief time in Magona. After he was unable to cross over to Spain, as he wished to do, he decided to go back to Africa again. (2) Doubtless at the inspiration of the martyr himself, he placed in the church of Magona some relics of St Stephen the martyr, which recently had come to light and which he had intended to transport to Spain.[3] (3) When this was done, straightaway the fire of His love was kindled, the fire which the Lord 'came to cast upon the earth' [Luke 12: 49] and which He wishes to blaze forth.[4] (4) Immediately our complacency heated up, and, as it is written, our hearts were 'burning by the way' [Luke 24: 32]. At one moment, zeal for the faith would fire

29 caritatis *PWz:* caritate *V*     ignis *P, trans. ante* quem Dominus *Vz:* ignes *W*
30 siquidem *PV:* quidem *W:* quippe *z*

83

illud fidei amburebat zelus, nunc spes salvandae multitudinis
erigebat.

5. Denique statim intercisa sunt etiam salutationis officia, et
non solum familiaritatis consuetudo divulsa est, sed etiam
5 noxia inveteratae species caritatis ad odium temporale, sed pro
aeternae salutis amore, translata est. (2) In omnibus plateis
adversus Iudaeos pugnae legis, in omnibus domibus fidei
proelia gerebantur.

6. Iudaeorum populus maxime cuiusdam Theodori auctori-
10 tate atque peritia nitebatur, qui non solum inter Iudaeos
verum etiam inter Christianos eiusdem oppidi, et censu et
honore saeculi praecipuus erat. (2) Siquidem apud illos legis
doctor et, ut ipsorum utar verbo, pater pateron fuit. (3) In
civitate autem cunctis curiae muniis exsolutis, et defensor iam
15 extiterat et etiam nunc patronus municipum habetur. (4)
Christiani autem, ut corde ita etiam et viribus humiles sed veri-
tatis robore superiores, patroni Stephani auxilium deprecabantur, donec utrique exercitus, cum iam diem certaminis
condixissent, datis tunc indutiis discesserunt.

20 7. Iudaeis id magnopere expetentibus ut scilicet Theodorus, in
cuius se omnis synagoga viribus acclinabat, ex Maioricensi
insula reverteretur, ad quam tunc forte visendae possessionis
gratia perrexerat. (2) Qui quidem statim ut ad eum missa
legatio est, remeans auctoritate sua multos terruit et non
25 extinxit sed paululum sopivit contentionis incendium. Maiore
siquidem ilico exardescens violentia etiam vicinum oppidum
fidei flamma corripuit. (3) Et ut illa Salomonis sententia
impleretur, 'Frater fratrem adiuvans exaltabitur sicut civitas
firma et alta', statuerunt multi famuli, Christi laborem itineris
30 minime recusantes, cunctas animi vires huic bello tradere.

8. Pendente igitur proelio, nos quidem qualia praeparaverimus

1 illud fidei amburebat *P*: illius fidei cor urebat *W*: illum in fide iam urebat *V*: illud
fide iam urebat *SG*: illum fide urebat *A*: illud fidei adurebat *C*    spes *PWC*: spe
*VSAG*    3 etiam *om. W*    4 consuetudo *om. P*    divulsa *WVz*: convulsa *P*
est *om. Vz*    5 odium *Vz*: otium *PW*    sed *om. W*    9 Theodori *om. W*
13 ipsorum *WVz*: eorum *P*    pater *om. PW*    pateron *PWVSG*: patheron *A*:
patrum *C*    14 muniis *PWz*: munus *V*    ex(s)olutis *Vz*: exsolvendis *P*: exso-
lutus *W*    15 et *om. WV*    patronus *PWVGC*: patruus *SA*    municipum *WV*:
municipii *SAG*: munipii *C, om. P*    habetur *PWVG*: habebatur *SA*: haberetur *C*
16 etiam *om. PC*    19 indutiis *PWSAC*: inditiis *V*: indiciis *G*    20 expetentibus *PWz*: expectantibus *V*    21 Maioricensi *PW*: Maioricense *V*: Minoricensi
*z*    22 tunc *om. V*    23 quidem *om. PW*

our hearts; at another moment, the hope of saving a multitude would spur us on.

5. In the end, even the obligation of greeting one another was suddenly broken off, and not only was our old habit of easy acquaintance disrupted, but the sinful appearance of our long-standing affection was transformed into temporary hatred, though for love of eternal salvation. (2) In every public place, battles were waged against the Jews over the Law, in every house struggles over the faith.[5]

6. The Jewish people relied particularly on the influence and knowledge of a certain Theodorus, who was pre-eminent in both wealth and worldly honour not only among the Jews, but also among the Christians of that town [Magona]. (2) Among the Jews he was a teacher of the Law and, if I may use their own phrase, the Father of Fathers.[6] (3) In the town, on the other hand, he had already fulfilled all the duties of the town council and served as *defensor*, and even now he is considered the *patronus* of his fellow citizens. (4) The Christians, however, humble in heart as well as physical strength, yet superior by the force of truth, prayed for the assistance of Stephen, their patron,[7] until the two armies separated, after they had agreed upon a day for their debate and concluded a truce for the present moment.

7. The Jews were eager for Theodorus, on whose strength the whole synagogue relied, to return from the island of Majorca, where, by chance, he had gone at the time to inspect an estate. (2) Indeed, as soon as an embassy was sent to him, he returned and frightened many people by his authority, and although he did not extinguish our ardour for the struggle, he did calm it for a little while. Blazing up suddenly with greater ferocity, the flame of faith also engulfed the neighbouring town [of Jamona]. (3) And that the saying of Solomon might be fulfilled, 'A brother helping a brother shall be raised up like a solid and lofty city' [Prov. 18: 19], many of Christ's servants decided to devote all the strength of their spirit to this war, not objecting in the least to the toil of a journey [to Magona].

8. Now the tract appended to this letter demonstrates the

26 ilico *om*. *PW*      27 et *om*. *P*      ut *om*. *W*      illa *Pz*: il *W*: illud *V*      sententia *om*. *V*      30 animi *PW*: animae *Vz*      huic bello tradere *om*. *W*      31 prae-paraverimus *PVz*: praeparavimus *W*

arma subditum huic epistulae commonitorium probat. (2)
Quod quidem non pro quorumdam instructione edi voluimus,
quippe qua penitus egemus et quam a Beatitudine vestra
magis speramus, sed ut animadverti possit non minimam nos
5   sollicitudinem secundum modulum possibilitatis nostrae
suscepti habuisse certaminis; (3) Christum vero cuius 'regnum
non in sermone sed in virtute est' nobis ne verbum quidem
proferentibus, suis omnia viribus consummasse, et absque ullo
sudore certaminis exercitui suo hanc quam nemo aut optare
10  audebat aut sperare poterat victoriam concessisse. (4) Iudaei
igitur exemplis se Machabaei temporis cohortantes, mortem
quoque pro defendendis legitimis suis desiderabant. (5) Itaque
non solum libros revolvere sed etiam sudes, saxa, iacula omniaque telorum genera ad synagogam conferre coepere, ut Chris-
15  tianorum aciem virtute Sancti Spiritus praemunitam, si ita res
posceret, etiam corporis viribus propulsarent.

**9.** Interea dum hi apparatus geruntur, magno quoque
altrinsecus studio futurum instruitur bellum, utrique exercitus
innumerabilibus atque absolutissimis somniis commonentur.
20  (2) Quorum si nullam penitus fecero mentionem, non minimam videbor partem divinae gloriae operuisse. (3) Si enim
sancti Apostoli Pauli somnium Lucas sacrae historiae scriptor
inseruit, dicens virum Macedonem astitisse in visione noctis,
orantem ut adiuvaretur ab eo, et hac Apostolum visione
25  praemonitum itineris alio destinati cursum ad Macedoniam
convertisse, quanto itaque Domini nostri Iesu Christi maior
gloria est, qui id minimis atque indignis famulis revelare dignatus est quod etiam beato Apostolo demonstratum scriptura
celare noluit. (4) Igitur brevitatis causa, ne Beatitudini vestrae
30  fastidium fortasse ingeratur, duo tantum somnia inseram.

**10.** Apud nos devota quaedam et religiosissima nomine Theodora, quae et virginitate corporis et religione propositi et

2 pro *om. W*    edi *om. W*    voluimus *PWAG*: volumus *VSC*    3 beatitudine *PVz*: magnitudine *W*    9 sudore *PWVGC*: labore *SA*    10 sperare
*PWz*: separare *V*    11 temporis *PWVGC*: temporibus *SA*    13–14 omniaque *PVz*: omnia *W*    14 coepere *PVz*: coeperunt *W*    15 sancti *om. PW*
16 corporis *PWVG*: corporeis *C, om. SA*    21 gloriae *WVz*: clementiae *P*  si
*PWz*: sic *V*    22 scriptor *W*: scripto *P, om. Vz*    23 dicens *PVz*: docens *W*
25 praemonitum *PWz*: praemunitum *V*    destinati *WVz*: declinati *P*    ad
Macedoniam *PWz*: de Macedonia *V*    26 itaque *Vz*: utique *W, om. P*
27 famulis *om. P*    28 etiam *om. P*    Apostolo *WVz*: Paulo *P*    29 noluit

kinds of weapons we prepared in advance as the battle loomed.
(2) It was certainly not for anyone's edification that we wished
this tract to be published (for in *that* we are utterly deficient and
hope rather to acquire *it* from your Blessedness), but that it
might be noticed that we showed considerable concern, in so
far as our abilities allowed, for the struggle that had been
engaged.[8] (3) But, in truth, Christ, whose 'kingdom dwells not
in talk but in power' [1 Cor. 4: 20], achieved everything with
His own forces and without us even uttering a word. Without
any sweat from the struggle, He granted His army this victory
which no one dared hope for and which no one could expect.
(4) The Jews meanwhile were exhorting one another with
examples from the time of the Maccabees, and, in defence of
their religion, they desired even death. (5) Thus, they began not
only to consult their sacred books, but also to gather stakes,
rocks, javelins, and all kinds of weapons into the synagogue, in
order to repulse the Christians by physical force, if the situation
demanded it, although our battle line was defended by the
power of the Holy Spirit.

9. Meanwhile, as these preparations were being made and the
future war was being planned on each side with great zeal, both
armies were forewarned by countless dreams that were
perfectly clear. (2) If I make absolutely no mention of them, I
will appear to have concealed no small part of the divine glory.
(3) For if Luke, the writer of sacred history, included the dream
of the holy Apostle Paul, reporting that a man from Macedonia
stood over him in a night vision and prayed that he be helped
by him, and forewarned by this vision, the Apostle changed the
course of his journey for Macedonia [Acts 16: 9–10], how much
greater is the glory of our Lord Jesus Christ, who deigned to
reveal to his most insignificant and most unworthy servants
that which was revealed to the blessed Apostle and which
scripture was unwilling to conceal. (4) Therefore, for the sake of
brevity and that your Blessedness may not find my account
tedious, I will include just two dreams.

10. There was among us a certain devout and very religious
woman with the name of Theodora, who, because of her

*PWz*: voluit *V*    30 ingeratur *PW*: gignatur *Vz*    31 devota *om. SA*    et
*W*: ac *SGC, om. PVA*

nominis etiam interpretatione typum portare ecclesiae meretur. (2) Vidit in visione noctis viduam quamdam nobilissimam ad me, qui non pro merito sed pro divini muneris largitate sacerdotio fungor, insertas litteris preces misisse, quibus
5 mihi cunctos agros suos ad seminandum suppliciter offerret. (3) Simili etiam somnio me quoque ultimum omnium peccatorum, ut me ad seminandum praecingerem, Christus commonere dignatus est. (4) Vidua enim quaedam altera nobilissima, quam synagogae speciem habuisse non dubium
10 est, me ut agros suos incultos susciperem eosque, quoniam tempus sementis surgeret, diligenter excolerem deprecabatur. (5) Quae est autem altera nobilissima vidua nisi illa quae Christum impie perimendo semetipsam crudelissime viduavit? (6) Hoc somnium utriusque unum est: ante triginta ferme
15 quam implerentur dies, et vidisse nos et, licet absolutionem eius ignoraremus, tamen fratribus indicasse manifestum est.
11. Apud Iudaeos quoque miro divinae dispensationis ordine ut et nominis Theodorae et officii mei in uno homine societas conveniret. (2) Theodorus, qui summus sacerdos perfidi populi
20 erat, somnium quod viderat non solum Iudaeis sed etiam propinquae cuidam matrifamilias primariae ipsius civitatis multisque etiam Christianis, ante non parvum quam impleretur tempus, his sermonibus propalavit: (3) 'Eunti mihi', inquit, 'secundum consuetudinem ad synagogam duodecim viri
25 manus obvias obtulerunt, dicentes, "Quo vadis? leo illic est." (4) Cum ego audito leonis nomine trepidare coepissem, locum tamen dum fugam paro unde introspicerem repperi, et vidi monachos illic mira suavitate psallentes. (5) Maior ilico mihi terror adiectus est, et nisi in cuiusdam Iudaei nomine Ruben
30 ingressus fuissem domum, et inde ad matrem propinquam cursu praepeti convolassem, nequaquam vim mortiferi terroris

1 interpretatione *PVz*: interpretationem *W*   portare *PVz*: cernere *W*   ecclesiae *om. W*   2 meretur *Pz*: mereretur *WV*   2–3 nobilissimam *om. W*
3–4 largitate *PVz*: dono *W*   4 litteris preces misisse *PW*: litteras pretermisisse *VSG*: litteras premisisse *AC*   5 cunctos *om. W*   offerret *WVz*: offerre *P*
6 somnio *PVz*: modo *W*   6–7 me quoque ultimum omnium peccatorum *om. W*   ut me ad seminandum praecingerem *PW*: me ad seminandum praecingere *SG:* ad seminandum praecingere *VAC*   7–8 et *ante* commonere *add. Vz*
8 nam *ante* vidua *add. P*   10 incultos *om. P*   quoniam *WVz*: quando *P*
11 surgeret *PW*: urgeret *Vz*   12 vidua *om. P*   13 impie *PVz*: impiae *W*
14 namque *ante* somnium *add. W*   nam *ante* utriusque *add. P*   15 implerentur *Vz*: impleretur *PW*   16 ignoraremus *PWz*: ignoremus *V*   tamen *PWz*: tum *V*

virginity, her religious way of life, and even the significance of her name ['gift of God'], could rightfully serve as a symbol of the church. (2) She saw in a night vision a certain very noble widow sending a request to me in the form of a letter, in which she humbly offered me all her fields to sow, although I occupy the priesthood not from merit, but from the bounty of divine favor. (3) By a similar dream, Christ also deigned to summon me as well, the last among all sinners, in order that I prepare myself for the sowing: (4) for another very noble widow, who without any doubt symbolized the synagogue, begged me [in the dream] to take over her untilled fields and to cultivate them carefully, since the season for sowing was close at hand. (5) Who then is the noble widow but that widow who, by impiously killing Christ, cruelly widowed herself?[9] (6) The dream is identical in each case. It is well established that I both saw the vision about thirty days before it was fulfilled and, although I knew nothing of its fulfilment, that I recounted it to the brethren.

**11.** Among the Jews also, by the wondrous ordering of the divine dispensation, the name 'Theodora' and my office were associated and united in one man. (2) Theodorus, the high priest of that faithless people, recounted a dream vision that he had seen not only to Jews, but in particular to a certain kinswoman, a distinguished matriarch of that town, and to many Christians as well. Some time before it was fulfilled, he recounted it with these words, (3) 'As I was going into the synagogue in my usual way,' he said, 'twelve men barred my path with outstretched hands, saying, "Where are you going? There is a lion in there." (4) Although I had begun to tremble at hearing the word "lion" and was getting ready to flee, none the less I searched out a spot from which I might peer in, and I saw monks inside singing with uncanny sweetness. (5) A greater terror was immediately aroused in me, and if I had not first entered the house of a certain Jew named Reuben, and from there raced headlong to the side of my married kinswoman, I could scarcely have escaped the force of that deadly terror.

18 Theodorae *PVz*: Theodori *W*      23 mihi *om. z*      24 secundum consuetudinem *om. Vz*      ad synagogam *PWA*: a synagoga *VSG*      25 obtulerunt *PVz*: dederunt *W*      26 ego *PWSAG*: ergo *VC*      27 paro *PWz*: puto *V*   29 Iudaei *om. VA*      31 praepeti *PW*: praecipiti *Vz*      vim *PWz*: curam *V*

evasissem. (6) Illa, inquam, me exanimem sinu suo confovens
et a discrimine pariter et metu eripuit.' (7) Hoc eius somnium
valde clarum est et interpretatione non indiget. (8) Quis enim
leo nisi ille 'de tribu Iuda, radix David'? Quae propinqua nisi
5    illa de qua scriptum est, 'una est propinqua mea'? (9) Illud
ergo solum videbatur obscurum, quod in domum Ruben
Iudaei cum a leone terreretur ingressus est. Quod quidem
nobis postmodum ab ipso leone, qui terruit ut salvaret, eviden-
tissime expositum est. Quod dehinc suo explicabimus loco.

10   **12.** Nunc autem, ut coeptae rei ordinem prosequar, maior ex
Iamonensi civitate ad profectionem parata famulorum Christi
multitudo convenit quam in ipso oppido putabatur consistere.
(2) Tantaque difficillimi itineris laborem alacritate confecit, ut
triginta milia passuum iucundius transvolaret quam si ad sub-
15   urbanum aliquod amoenissimum ad convivia epulari vocaretur. (3) Igitur Magonam pervenimus, statimque ego missis
clericis adventum meum Iudaeis nuntiavi, et ut ad ecclesiam
succedere dignarentur poposci. (4) Illi autem inopinatum
nobis nuntium remittentes, mandaverunt ecclesiam sibi (ne,
20   credo, polluerentur) ingredi die eadem non oportere, esse enim
diem sabbati, cuius festivitatem si ullis actibus corrupissent,
summum transgressionis facinus incurrerent. (5) Rursus ego
expetivi ut me ad synagogam, si mallent, opperirentur, quoniam quidem ipsis ingressus ecclesiae pollutio videretur; non
25   utique eos a nobis in die sabbati ad opus servile compelli, (6)
futurum autem esse modestissimum de lege conflictum, nec
excitandas lites sed fabulas esse miscendas, aut, si non astute
certamen fugerent sed simplicem afferrent excusationem,
ostenderent praeceptum quo in die festo sermonem his con-
30   ferre prohibitum sit. (7) Ad haec cum illi in omnibus contradic-
tionem obstinatissimam retulissent, tandem illius leonis terrore

1 evasissem *PW*¹: evaseram *W*²*Vz*    inquam *Vz*: inquit *P, om. W*        2 et *post*
confovens *om. V*    a *ante* metu *add. VG*        5 est *ante* propinqua *om. P*
6 domum *PW*: domo *Vz*        8 postmodum *PVz*: postea *W*        10 prosequar
*PWGC*: persequar *VSA*    maior *om. Vz*        11 parata *PW*: paratam *z, om. V*
12 quam *PW*: quae *Vz*    putabatur *PVz*: putabat *W*        14 transvolaret *PWV*:
pervolaret *z*    quam si *PWz*: quasi *V*        14–15 suburbanum *WVz*: urbanum *P*
15–16 convivia epulari vocaretur *Vz*: convivii (a)epulas evocaretur *PW*        17 et
*om. WC*        20 die eadem *om. PW*        21 si ullis actibus *PW*: suis illi actibus
*Vz*        22 summum transgressionis facinus *om. Vz*    incurrerent *W*: incurrissent
*P, om. Vz*        23 me *om. PW*        23–4 quoniam quidem *WVC*: quandoqui-
dem *P*: quamquidem *z*        24 ipsis *om. V*        25 festo *post* die *add. V*

(6) She soothed me, breathless, at her bosom, and rescued me from both danger and fear.' (7) His dream is perfectly clear and in need of no interpretation. (8) For who is the lion, but that 'Lion of the tribe of Judah, the Root of David' [Rev. 5: 5]? Who is that kinswoman, if not that one of whom it is written, 'My kinswoman is but one'?[10] (9) Therefore, one point alone seemed obscure, namely that he entered the house of a Jew called Reuben when he was terrified by the Lion. This was indeed explained very plainly to us afterwards by the very Lion who terrified him, in order that he might save him. We will treat this matter later in its proper place.

**12.** Now, however, to proceed with my narrative, a throng of Christ's servants, greater than was thought to reside in that town, gathered together and prepared for the departure from Jamona. (2) Although it was a very arduous journey, they completed it with such speed that they flew over the thirty miles more light-heartedly than if they were being invited to a banquet at some beauty spot outside the town. (3) And so we arrived at Magona.[11] Immediately, I dispatched some clerics to announce my arrival to the Jews and requested that they do us the honour of entering the church. (4) They, however, sent back to us an unexpected message, announcing that it was inappropriate for them to enter a church on that day, lest, I suppose, they be polluted, since it was the Sabbath. If they should corrupt its observance by any actions, they would be committing a very serious, criminal transgression. (5) Again I made a request, to the effect that they should wait for me at the synagogue if they preferred, since entry into the church seemed a source of pollution, and in any case they were not being forced by us into any menial labour on the Sabbath. (6) On the contrary, the dispute concerning the Law was to be thoroughly calm, and there should be no stirring up quarrels, but rather a sharing of views in discussion. If, on the other hand, they were not avoiding the debate through a ruse, but were offering a genuine excuse, then let them show us the rule by which it was prohibited for them to engage in discussion on a holy day.[12] (7) Although they replied by stubbornly contradicting me on every point, they were in the end driven by terror of that Lion to

27 excitandas *PVz*: exercitandas *W*    28 sed *PWz*: et *V*    excusationem *PVz*: accusationem *W*    29 quo *Wz*: quod *PV*    in *om. P*    festo *om. V*    his *om. W*    31 retulissent *WVz*: pertulissent *P*

compulsi, ad domum in qua hospitio accesseram confluxerunt.
(8) Ibi ego, 'quaeso', inquam, 'fratres, quare quasi adversum
latrones praesertim in civitate Romanis legibus subdita,
acervos saxorum omniaque armorum genera congregastis? (9)
5 Nos codices ad docendum detulimus, vos ad occidendum
gladios ac vectes. (10) Nos acquirere cupimus, vos perdere
desideratis. Non est, quantum arbitror, aequum ut tam varia
lite alterutrum laboremus. Vos vero, ut video, sititis nostrum
sanguinem, nos vestram salutem.' (11) Ad haec illi paululum
10 territi negavere factum, nostrisque affirmantibus ita rem se
habere, etiam cum iureiurando renitebantur. (12) Tum ego, ut
nodum coeptae contentionis absciderem, 'Ubi res', inquam,
'oculis probari potest, iuratione quid opus est? (13) Eamus
igitur ad synagogam et utrum periurio an veritate vestra nitatur
15 assertio vobismetipsis testibus comprobabitur.'
13. Pergere igitur ad synagogam coepimus et hymnum
Christo per plateam ex multitudine laetitiae canebamus. (2)
Psalmus autem, quem mira iucunditate etiam Iudaeorum
populus decantabat, hic fuit, 'Periit memoria eorum cum
20 strepitu et Dominus in aeternum permanet'. (3) Sed antequam
ad synagogam perveniremus, quaedam Iudaeae mulieres
(ordinatione, credo, Domini) audaciam praesumentes, ut
scilicet nostrorum lenitas incitaretur, lapides in nos ex superiori loco immanissimos iactare coeperunt. (4) Qui, mirum
25 dictu, cum super confertissimam multitudinem grandinis
instar deciderent, neminem nostrum non solum ictu sed nec
tactu quidem vexavere. (5) Hic agnis suis leo ille terribilis mansuetudinem paululum abstulit. (6) Omnes siquidem frustra
reclamantibus nobis saxa corripiunt, et pastoris commonitione
30 posthabita, cum unum consilium cunctis zelus potius Christi
quam ira suggereret, lupos cornibus impetendos censuerunt,
quamvis hoc illius qui solus verus et bonus pastor est nutu
factum esse nulli dubium sit. (7) Denique, ne cruentam gregi

1 qua *PVz*: quam *W*    accesseram *PVz*: successeram *W*    2 ibi *PVz*: ubi *W*
quare *om. V*    3 subdita *PVz*: subditam *W*    5–6 nos codices . . . vectes *om.*
*V*    5 docendum *Pz*: legendum *W, om. V*    6 ac vectes *A*: acutes *P*: et
vectes *WSGC, om. V*    9 haec *PWz*: hoc *V*    illi *om. z*    10 negavere
*WVz*: necavere *P*    nostrisque *PWz*: nostris *V*    rem *PWz*: esse *V*
15 vobismetipsis *PWz*: nobismetipsis *V*    comprobabitur *PVz*: comprobatur *W*
19 periit *WVz*: perit *P*    20 strepitu *PVSAG*: sonitu *WC*    22 Domini *Pz*:
Dei *WV*    audaciam *PWV*: audacia *z*    23–4 superiori *PWV*: superiore *z*

gather at the house where I was being lodged. (8) There I said, 'I ask you, brothers, why, particularly in a city subject to Roman laws, you have gathered together heaps of stones and all sorts of arms as if you faced brigands? (9) We brought books in order to instruct; you brought swords and clubs to commit murder. (10) We wish to increase; you desire to destroy. In my judgement, our struggle is not on an equal footing and our conflict is very different on the two sides. As I see it, you thirst for our blood, while we thirst for your salvation.' (11) They were a little frightened at these words and denied the fact of the matter, and when we affirmed that this was the case, they even began to resist with an oath.[13] (12) Then, to cut the knot of contention, I said, 'When the matter can be proved with one's eyes, what need is there for an oath? (13) Let's go to the synagogue, and it will be confirmed with yourselves as witnesses whether your assertion rests on perjury or truth.'

**13.** Then we set out for the synagogue, and along the way we began to sing a hymn to Christ in our abundance of joy. (2) Moreover, the psalm was 'Their memory has perished with a crash and the Lord endures forever' [Ps. 9: 7–8], and the throng of Jews also began to sing it with a wondrous sweetness.[14] (3) But before we reached the synagogue, certain Jewish women (by God's arrangement, I suppose) acted recklessly, and, doubtless to rouse our people from their gentleness, began to throw huge stones down on us from a higher spot. (4) Although the stones, marvellous to relate, fell like hail over a closely packed crowd, not only was none of our people harmed by a direct hit, but not one was even touched. (5) At this point, that terrible Lion took away for a short while the mildness from his lambs. (6) While I protested in vain, they all snatched up stones, and neglecting their shepherd's warning, since they were united in a plan suggested more by zeal for Christ than by anger, they decided that the wolves had to be attacked with horns, although no one could doubt that this was done with the approval of Him who alone is the true and good shepherd. (7) Finally, lest it seem that He had granted His flock a bloody

---

24 iactare *Vz*: iacere *PW*  26 deciderent *PWz*: descenderent *V*  nostrum
*PWA*: nostrorum *VSG*  27 hic *PWV*: his *z*  27–8 mansuetudinem *om. W*
28 siquidem *Vz*: quidem *PW*  frustra *om. Vz*  32 verus *om. V*

suo videretur praestitisse victoriam, nemo Iudaeorum se contactum saltem fuisse, ne pro invidia quidem, ut mos est, simulavit. (8) Sane quoniam omnimodis debemus vitare mendacium, unus ex omni Christianorum numero inventus est,

5 qui Achar illi similis esse vellet qui sub Iesu Nave quaedam de anathemate spolia concupivit. (9) Nam servus cuiusdam Christiani, sicut ipse post compulsus est confiteri, non Christi illuc sed praedae amore adtractus advenerat. (10) Qui solus, dum aliquid a synagoga diripere concupiscit, in lapidem offensionis

10 incurrit. Quidam enim nostrorum quasi adversus Iudaeum saxum iniecit, quod capiti eius inlisum ut capitis sui id est Christi meminisset admonuit. (11) Quod vulnus licet periculosum non fuerit tamen et illum rapinae suae confiteri concupiscentiam compulit et cunctos ne similiter laberentur

15 praesenti terruit ultione. (12) Igitur posteaquam Iudaeis cedentibus synagoga potiti sumus, nullus ex ea quicquam non dico abstulit sed nec cogitavit diripere. (13) Omnia eius ornamenta, exceptis tamen libris atque argento, cum ipsa pariter ignis absumpsit. Libros enim sanctos ne apud Iudaeos iniuriam

20 paterentur nos abstulimus; argentum vero ne vel de praedatione nostra vel de suo dispendio quererentur ipsis reddidimus. 14. Eversa itaque cunctis Iudaeis stupentibus synagoga, ad ecclesiam cum hymnis perreximus, et auctori victoriae nostrae gratias referentes, effusis fletibus poscebamus ut vera perfidiae

25 antra Dominus expugnaret et tenebrosorum pectorum infidelitas coargueretur a lumine.
15. Nec ulla in effectu mora, postera siquidem die, ut congruentia nominum in omnibus servaretur, Ruben quidam Iudaeus a Domino ut primogenitus omnium constitueretur

30 electus est. (2) Nam clamore sanctissimo laetificans corda cunctorum, absolvi se a vinculis Iudaicae superstitionis deprecabatur. (3) Statimque 'primogenitus Iacob' factus, signum salutare suscepit, et exinde nostris adhaerens lateribus atque

---

2 pro *om. P*     3 vitare *PW*: evitare *Vz*     5 Achar *Vz*: Acham *P*: Accaz *W*
9 concupiscit *PVz*: concupivit *W*     10 enim *PWz*: vero *V*     11 saxum
*PWz*: lapidem *V*     15 praesenti *PVz*: praesentes *W*     16 synagoga
*PVW²z*: synagogam *V¹*, synagoga *V²*     ex *om. W*     18 tamen *PVz*: tantum
*W*     pariter *PWz*: pariete *V*     19 enim *om. V*     20 vel *om. P*
20–1 praedatione *P*: praeda *WVz*     24 fletibus *PWz*: precibus *V*
27 effectu *PWVGC*: affectu *SA*     28 quidam *WVz*: quidem *P*     32 primogenitus *Wz*: primitivus *PV*     33 et *om. VSA*     adhaerens *om. V*

94

victory, not one of the Jews pretended even to have been touched, not even to stir up ill will, as usually happens. (8) Admittedly, since we must in every way avoid deceit, one man out of the entire number of Christians was discovered who desired to be like that Achan who, under Joshua son of Nun, coveted spoils from the forbidden things [Josh. 7: 1]. (9) For the slave of a certain Christian, as he himself was later forced to confess, had come to that place, drawn not by love of Christ, but by love of plunder. (10) He alone was greedy to steal something from the synagogue, and he was struck by a stone for his offence. In fact, someone from our group threw the stone, though he was aiming at a Jew, but it struck the slave on the head and admonished him to recall his true head, namely Christ. (11) Although the wound was not dangerous, it both forced him to confess his greedy desire for theft, and, by its obvious retribution, it put fear in everyone else lest they lapse in a similar way. (12) Therefore, after the Jews had retreated and we had gained control of the synagogue, no one, I won't say, 'stole' anything, but no one even considered 'looting' anything! (13) Fire consumed the synagogue itself and all of its decorations, with the exception of the books and silver.[15] We removed the sacred books so that they wouldn't suffer harm among the Jews, but the silver we returned to them so that there would be no complaining either about us taking spoils or about them suffering losses.[16]

14. And so, while all the Jews stood stupified at the destruction of the synagogue, we set out for the church to the accompaniment of hymns and, giving thanks to the author of our victory, we poured forth our tears and beseeched the Lord to lay siege to the true dens of their unbelief and to expose to the light the faithlessness of their dark hearts.

15. Nor was there any delay in the accomplishment, for on the following day, a certain Jew called Reuben was chosen by the Lord (that appropriate names be preserved in all matters) to be made the first-born of them all. (2) For he delighted the hearts of all with a most holy cry, praying that he be released from the chains of Jewish superstition. (3) And without delay he became the 'first-born of Jacob' [Gen. 35: 23] and received the sign of salvation. From that moment he remained close to our sides

consiliis, obstinatissimam cunctorum duritiam nobiscum increpabat.

**16.** Triduum, ni fallor, emensum est in quo et nostri in orationibus et Iudaei in perfidia perstiterunt. (2) Post id venit
5 Theodorus, multitudinis suae agmine circumsaeptus, ad locum in quo soli synagogae parietes (qui postea a Iudaeis credentibus subversi sunt) superesse videbantur; ad quem locum etiam Christianorum mecum pariter multitudo convenit. (3) Ibi Theodorus cum audacter de lege contendens
10 omnia quae obiciebantur irrideret atque perverteret, populus Christianus videns quia verbis superari non posset humanis, auxilium de caelo imploravit. (4) Omnes itaque pariter conclamantes cum summo unitae vocis fragore dixerunt, 'Theodore, credas in Christum!' (5) Mira indulgentissimi Domini
15 misericordia, adhuc parva petebantur, et iam maiora concesserat. (6) Immo non mirum est de Omnipotente miraculum! Ipse enim virtutem clamoris huius in auribus Iudaeorum commutavit, qui olim effecit ut quattuor leprosi regis Syriae qui Samariam obsederat castris potirentur; et qui per Gedeon
20 Madianitarum agmina conturbavit deditque trecentis eius viris ingentem sine labore victoriam, efficiens per terrorem ut mutuis hostium multitudo vulneribus prosterneretur. (7) Ita et nunc ista vox longe aliter a circumstantibus Iudaeis suscepta est, quam a nostris emittebatur. Omnes enim putavere dictum,
25 'Theodorus in Christum credidit!' Itaque aestimantes principem perfidiae suae ad Christi fidem fuisse conversum, cuncti pariter trepidi; ubi timor non erat, terrebantur. (8) Mulieres eorum sparsis crinibus concurrentes cum ferali ululatu nomen Theodori repetitis vocibus accusabant dicentes, 'O Theodore,
30 quid fecisti?' (9) Viri autem alii ad devios saltus et fissuras montium confugere, alii per ipsius oppidi angiportus discurrebant, locum in quo delitescerent invenire cupientes. (10) Ipse

1 duritiam *PWz*: duritiem *V*    2 increpabat *Pz*: increpat *WV*    4 perstiterunt *WVz*: persisterunt *P*    id *PWz*: haec *V*    6 postea *PW*: post haec *Vz* a *om. PV*    7 subversi sunt *PWz*: subversis *V*    8 mecum *om. V*    pariter *om. W*    9 ibi *WVz*: ubi *P*    10 irrideret *PVz*: derideret *W*    11 quia *PWz*: quod *V*    13 unitae *PVz*: intentae *W*    dixerunt *PVz*: dicebant *W* 14 Christum *Vz*: Christo *PW*    15 petebantur *PWVA*: petebatur *SGC*    et iam maiora *WGC*: etiam maiora *PVS*: et maiora iam *A*    16 mirum *om. V* 17 ipse enim *PW*: ipse etenim *V*: is etenim *z*    17–18 commutavit *WVz*: commutabit *P*    19 Gedeon *PWz*: Geon *V*    20 eius *om. PW*    23 vox *PWz*: nox *V*    25 in Christum *WVz*: Christo *P*    aestimantes *PW*: existi-

and our counsels, and along with us reviled the stubborn hard-heartedness of all [the Jews].

**16.** A span of three days passed, if I am not mistaken, in which our people persevered in prayers and the Jews persevered in faithlessness. (2) After that, Theodorus, hedged round with a contingent of his followers, came to the spot where only the walls of the synagogue, which were later pulled down by Jewish converts, could be seen to survive. In that spot a throng of Christians also gathered along with me. (3) There Theodorus debated boldly about the Law, and after he had mocked and twisted all of our objections, the Christian throng, seeing that he could not be vanquished by human arguments, prayed for assistance from heaven. (4) They all shouted together and cried in thunderous unison, 'Theodorus, believe in Christ!' (5) From our most indulgent Lord's marvellous mercy, small favours were still being sought, and He had already granted greater ones. (6) But no! A miracle from the Omnipotent is no 'miraculous' thing! He Himself transformed the import of this shouting in the ears of the Jews, He who once brought it about that four lepers should seize the camp of the King of Syria, who had laid seige to Samaria [2 Kgs. 7], and He who routed through Gideon the battle lines of the Midianites, and who granted a great, effortless victory to three hundred of his men, bringing it about through terror that a multitude of the enemy should kill one another with self-inflicted wounds [Judg. 7: 19–22]. (7) Similarly in the present instance, the Jewish bystanders mis-interpreted the phrase spoken by our people, for they all thought they had heard, 'Theodorus has believed in Christ!' As a result, since they all thought that the leader of their faithless-ness had been converted to faith in Christ, they were all equally afraid, and where there was no cause for fear, they were terrified. (8) Racing together with dishevelled hair and wild howling, their women assailed Theodorus with repeated cries, 'Theodorus, what have you done?' (9) As for the men, however, some fled to pathless groves and mountain ravines, while others scattered through the streets of the town in their desire to discover a place where they could hide. (10) Theodorus himself

mantes *Vz*      26 fuisse *om. W*      28 concurrentes *PWz*: occurrentes *V* 30 fissuras *PWSGC*: fixuras *VA*      31 montium *WVz*: petrarum *P*      confugere *PWVGC*: fugere *SA*      autem *ante* per *add. W*      31–2 discurrebant *PVz*: con-currebant *W*

Theodorus stupore perculsus divinam sententiam in plebe sua cernebat impleri, 'Fugit impius nemine persequente'. Sed tamen non 'nemine'! Persequebatur enim eos ille leo terribilis qui de synagogae loco, sicut Theodoro fuerat revelatum, per
5 monachos rugitum emiserat, quo resistentes tremefecit inimicos. (11) Stabat igitur Theodorus in loco prorsus eodem quo ei pridem per somnium terror leonis fuerat iniectus, et cum causam tantae trepidationis inquireret et nomen solummodo nostri leonis audiret, nullam illic, sicut verebatur, feritatem
10 videns, tantum psallentes monachos intuebatur. Et ab omni suorum multitudine destitutus, atque elabi parans etiam ipse pedum viam prospiciebat. (12) Quem cum horribili formidine adprehensum, et non solum colore vultus verum etiam vocis officio destitutum, Ruben ille sanctissimus aspexisset, propere
15 accessit et trementem blando sermone compellans ad fidem Christi cohortabatur; atque ingerens ei pro suffragio metus suae credulitatis exemplum, domum fidei suae ad quam a leonis pavore confugeret quodammodo patefacere videbatur. (13) Verumtamen ut et nos universa fideliter narremus et vos,
20 qui non eloquii ornatum sed veritatem quaeritis, libentius audiatis, ipsius Ruben verba inserens nihil ex simplicitate dictorum eius subtraham. (14) Aiebat enim, 'Quid times, domine Theodore? Si vis certe et securus et honoratus et dives esse, in Christum crede, sicut et ego credidi. (15) Modo tu stas
25 et ego cum episcopis sedeo. Si credideris, tu sedebis et ego ante te stabo.' (16) Hos Theodorus sermones alta mente suscipiens, ad nos ait, 'Faciam quod vultis. Tenete', inquit, 'promissionem hanc, sed permittite mihi ut prius alloquar plebem meam, ut maiorem conversionis meae etiam ex reliquis possim habere
30 mercedem.' (17) Haec eius sponsio cum inaestimabili cunctorum exultatione suscepta est. (18) Alii in eum amabiliter irruentes, os ipsius osculis et colla mulcebant; alii eum ulnis

2 cernebat *Vz*: cernens *W*: videbat *P*     impleri *WVz*: impletam *P*     persequente *PWz*: persequenti *V*     sed *om. W*     3 enim *om. W*     5 quo *Vz*: quos *PW* resistentes *PWV*: resistente *z*     tremefecit *Vz*: fecit *PW*     6 in *ante* quo *add. PW* 8 causam *PWV*: causas *z*     9 sicut *WV*: sic *P*: ut *z*     verebatur *PWz*: ferebatur *V*     13 verum *WVz*: sed *P*     14 propere *Vz*: propter *P*: prope *W* 15 accessit *PW*: accedit *Vz*     21 inserens *PVz*: inferens *W*     22 times *PWV*: timeas *z*     23 et *ante* securus *om. VA*     25 tu *ante* credideris *add. VS* 28 ut *ante* prius *om. z*     29 reliquis *PWz*: reliquiis *V*     30 in(a)estimabili *PWz*: inextimabili *V*     31 exultatione *WVz*: gaudio *P*     32 ipsius *WVA*:

was stunned and shocked, and he perceived that among his people the divine judgement was being fulfilled: 'The wicked man runs away with no one in pursuit' [Prov. 28: 1]. But wait, it was not 'no one'! That terrible Lion was pursuing them, who from the site of the synagogue, as had been revealed to Theodorus, had unleashed through the monks the roar by which He put fear in our resisting enemies. (11) Thus, Theodorus was standing on the very same spot where previously in his dream he had been smitten with terror of the Lion, and although he searched for the source of his great anxiety and heard only the name of our Lion, he saw nothing fierce there, as he feared he would. All he saw was monks singing psalms. And since he had been abandoned by the whole multitude of his people and he too was preparing to slip away, he began to look for an escape route on foot. (12) Now when Reuben, that most holy man, had caught sight of Theodorus, gripped with terrible fear, and not only pale but unable even to speak, he quickly approached him, addressing the trembling man with coaxing words and encouraging him toward faith in Christ. And by offering him the example of his own faith as a refuge from fear, he seemed somehow to open up the house of his faith, to which Theodorus was fleeing from fear of the Lion. (13) Still, in order that we may recount every detail faithfully and that you may listen eagerly, you who seek not rhetorical adornment, but the truth, I will include the words of Reuben himself and suppress none of the frankness of his speech. (14) Reuben said, 'What do you fear, Lord Theodorus? If you truly wish to be safe and honoured and wealthy, believe in Christ, just as I too have believed. (15) Right now you are standing, and I am seated with bishops; if you should believe, you will be seated, and I will be standing before you.' (16) After pondering these words deep in his mind, Theodorus replied to us, 'I shall do what you wish,' he said, 'Accept this promise, but allow me first to address my people, so that I may reap a greater reward for my conversion by the conversion of the others as well.' (17) His pledge was received by everyone with incalculable joy. (18) Some ran to him affectionately and caressed his face and neck with kisses, others

ipsum *PSG*: eius *C*     colla mulcebant *Vz*: collum mulcebant *W*: mollibus amplexibus demulcebant *P*     eum *om. P*

mollibus complectebantur; alii autem dexteram dexterae adiungere aut sermonem conserere gestiebant. (19) Perrexit igitur Theodorus ad atrium suum quamlibet officio nostrorum laetus, tamen anxietate non penitus carens. Nam licet in
5   domum Ruben per promissionem suam iam videretur ingressus, tamen etiam nunc trepidus erat, quia necdum ad propinquam pervenerat, quae eum post triduum materno suscepit sinu et ab omni perturbatione trepidationis absolvit. (20) Nos autem ad ecclesiam cum hymnis ex more perreximus can-
10  tantes et psallentes, 'Benedictus est Pater misericordiarum et Deus totius consolationis', qui dedit capiti nostro aquam et oculis nostris fontem lacrimarum, ut ploraremus vulneratos populi nostri.'

17. Peractis siquidem mysteriis ecclesiam egressi, non mini-
15  mam in occursum nostrum Iudaeorum multitudinem convenisse inspeximus, (2) qui omnes unanimiter deprecabantur ut Christi characterem a me, licet indigno pastore, susciperent. (3) Reversi itaque ad ecclesiam, et misericordi Domino gratias referentes, ilico in frontibus eorum signum salutis impres-
20  simus.

18. Quae autem cum his, qui ad silvas sive ad antra confugerant, Christi virtute gesta sint, quae lingua effabitur? praesertim cum unusquisque eorum propriam conversionis suae habeat historiam. (2) Sicut itaque impossibile nobis est omnia
25  dicere, sic ingratum cuncta praeterire. (3) Quapropter unum Christi miraculum, quod tamen a fidelissimis probatissimisque viris comperimus, precibus vestris adiutus evolvam. (4) Duo quidam primarii Iudaeorum, id est Meletius, Theodori frater, et Innocentius, qui Hispaniarum cladem nuper fugiens
30  cum famulis suis ad hanc insulam venerat, sicut ipsi etiam nunc cum sacramentorum terribili interpositione confirmant, ad unam speluncam vel potius rupem convenerunt, associantibus se duobus quibusdam Iudaeis humili loco ortis, qui

1 complectebantur *WVz*: amplectebantur *P*    autem *WVz*: aut *P*    2 conserere *PWVGC*: conferre *SA*    3 igitur *om. SAG*    5 domum *PWVSG*: domo *AC*    videretur *PW*: veniretur *Vz*    6 etiam *om. z*    6–7 propinquam *PWz*: propinquum *V*    9–10 cantantes et psallentes *om. Vz*    10 deus *ante* pater *add. PW*    11 deus *PWz*: dominus *V*    14 sumus *post* egressi *add. W*    16 qui *om. Vz*    18 et *om. W*    19–20 impressimus *PWz*: impinximus *V*    21 ad *ante* antra *om. SA*    21–2 confugerant *PVz*: confugere *W*    22 sint *PVGC*: sunt *WSA*    22–3 praesertim *om. W*    28 quidam *WVz*: quidem *P*    29 Hispaniarum *V*: Ispaniarum *W*: Spaniarum *Pz*

embraced him in gentle arms, while still others longed to join right hands with him or to engage him in conversation. (19) And so Theodorus set out for his own home, happy at every sign of affection from our people, but nevertheless not completely free of anxiety, for although he seemed by now to have come to the house of Reuben by making his promise, none the less he was still at that point frightened, since he had not yet come to his kinswoman, who after three days took him to her maternal bosom and freed him from all confusion and fear. (20) We, on the other hand, set out for the church to the usual accompaniment of hymns, chanting and singing: 'Blessed is the Father of Mercies and the God of all Consolation' [2 Cor. 1: 3], who granted water for our heads and a font of tears for our eyes, in order that we might lament the wounded among our people [Jer. 9: 1].

**17.** After the completion of our holy rites, we left the church and observed that a good-sized crowd of Jews had gathered to meet us. (2) All of them with singleness of spirit pleaded that they might receive the symbol of Christ from me, unworthy shepherd that I am. (3) So we went back into the church, gave thanks to our merciful God, and there on the spot marked the sign of salvation on their foreheads.

**18.** Now what tongue can speak forth the things which, by the power of Christ, befell those who fled into forests or caves? Especially since each one of them has his own personal history of conversion. (2) However, just as it is impossible for me to say everything, so too will it be ungratifying for me to pass over everything. (3) Therefore, with the aid of your prayers, I shall unfold one of Christ's miracles, which we learned from men who are very trustworthy and of proven character. (4) Two leading men among the Jews were Meletius, the brother of Theodorus, and Innocentius, who had recently fled from the slaughter in Spain and had come to this island accompanied by his servants.[17] As they themselves will still confirm today with an awe-inspiring oath, they arrived at a cave, or rather a rocky outcrop, with two Jews of humble birth who joined up with

fugiens *PWA*: effugiens *VSGC*     30 famulis *WVAC*: familiis *PSG*     sicut *PVz*: sicuti *W*     32 convenerunt *PVz*: convenerant *W*     33 duobus *om. W* ortis *PVz*: hostis *W*

istos communis fugae principes legerant. (5) Igitur cum in loco eodem trepidi anhelantesque paululum resedissent, duos illos, qui aetate alacres et audaces erant, quasi explorandi gratia ad oppidum remittentes, soli derelicti sunt ibi. (6) Tunc prior
5 Meletius, 'Quid est hoc,' inquit, 'frater, quod verbum, sicut docet religio nostra, blasphemum avellere a corde meo nequeo? Ex quo enim fratrem meum fuisse conversum Christianorum populus inclamavit, nihil mihi aliud in corde suggeritur nisi hoc verbum, mihi usque ad hunc diem penitus
10 ignoratum: "Christe, in nomine tuo." Quantoque magis hoc propulsare ab animo meo nitor, tanto violentius tenaciusque inhaerescit.' (7) Ad haec Innocentius, 'Non', inquit, 'frustra hic sermo, quem neque cor tuum, ut apud cunctos probatissimum est, antea cogitavit neque os umquam protulit, hoc praesertim
15 tempore menti tuae, ut asseris, tam violenter insertus est. Ex Deo hoc esse arbitror. Verumtamen elabora, obsecro, et fabulis alio declinatis interpellationem molestae cogitationis expelle.' (8) Tunc Meletius ita obstrepere et confusis clamoribus personare coepit, ut eum cum sua mente luctari non solum
20 nutibus vultus sed etiam totius corporis indicio Innocentius cerneret. (9) Quod posteaquam ne parum quidem proficere intellexit, adiecit etiam illud, ut verba quaedam profana ac turpia loqueretur; et nunc naribus corrugatis aerem sorbens, inhonestos strepitus promeret; nunc foetidis risibus cachin-
25 naret. (10) Sed haec ab animo eius nomen Christi extinguere nequivit insania, quia iam cunctas eius medullas sanitatis ignis pervaserat. (11) 'Quid ago,' inquit, 'Innocenti frater? In contrarium remedia ista vertuntur. Abolitionem mihi nominis Christi nec scurrilitate verborum nec ipsis possum obsceni
30 sonitus extorquere blasphemiis. Alium siquidem, mihi crede, sentio, qui cordis mei auribus, quas frustra obstruere nitor, Christi nomen ingerere incessabili clamore non desinit.' (12) His Meletii verbis talia Innocentius retulit, 'Fratrem tuum,

1 legerant *WVSGC*: elegerant *PA*    2 eodem *PWz*: eorum *V*    paululum *Pz*: paulum *V*    resedissent *WVz*: residissent *P*    4 remittentes *PVz*: renitentes *W*    10 ignoratum *PVz*: incognitum *W*    12 inhaerescit *PVz*: inhaeret *W* est *post* non *add. V*    13 neque cor *PWz*: in cor *V*    14 est *om. z*    os *om. Vz*    tuum *post* os *add. P*    hoc *PWV¹z*: hic *V²*    15 tempore *om. Vz* 16 fabulis *PWVGC*: famulis *SA*    17 interpellationem *PVz*: interpolationem *W* 18 ita *om. W*    19 personare *PVz*: clamare *W*    21 ne *om. P*    22 et *ante* adiecit *add. V*    ac *Wz*: et *PV*    24–5 cachinnaret *PWz*: cachinnarent *V* 25 animo *P¹Vz*: anima *P²W*    27 ago *PWz*: ego *V*    29 obsceni *Vz*: ob-

them and had chosen them as leaders in the general flight. (5) After they had sat in that spot for a little while, trembling and out of breath, they sent the other two men, who were young and ready for action, back to the town to explore. They were left there alone. (6) Then Meletius began, 'Why is it, brother, that I can't expel from my heart a phrase which, as our religion teaches, is blasphemy? From the moment when the crowd of Christians cried out that my brother had been converted, nothing has arisen in my heart but this phrase which was completely unknown to me until today: "Christ, in your name". And the more I struggle to drive it from my spirit, the more fiercely and stubbornly it sticks there.' (7) Innocentius replied, 'It is not without purpose that this phrase has been, as you claim, so forcibly implanted in your mind at this particular time, even though your heart—a very reliable one in all people's opinion—has never thought of it nor your mouth ever uttered it. I consider it to be from God. None the less, exert yourself, I beg of you, and setting aside this idle talk, drive out the intruding, hateful thought.' (8) Then Meletius began to shriek and utter garbled cries in such a way that Innocentius perceived that he was struggling within his mind, not only from the shaking of his head but from the appearance of his whole body. (9) But when he realized that this was absolutely no help, he also added that Meletius should utter certain vile profanities. At one moment, he would wrinkle his nostrils, suck in some air, then force the air out with indecent noises. At another moment, he would cackle with disgusting laughter. (10) But this madness was unable to extinguish the name of Christ from his mind, since already the fire of good health had penetrated to the depth of his marrow. (11) 'What am I doing, brother Innocentius? Those remedies are being twisted contrariwise. I can't banish Christ's name with profanity, nor can I expel it with foul-sounding blasphemies. Indeed, I am conscious, trust me, of another sound, which does not stop forcing Christ's name with its relentless clamour on the ears of my heart, though I try in vain to block them.' (12) To the words of Meletius, Innocentius spoke as follows, 'The Christian throng

scenis $P^1$ W: obsceno $P^2$     30 crede C: credis PWSAG: credi V     31 qui PWz: quod V     mei om. z     32 desinit PVz: desistit W     33 talia WVz: alia P

Theodorum, doctrina, honore, aetate maiorem ad fidem
Christi conversum his auribus audientibus plebs Christiana
testata est. (13) Poteritne fieri ut non etiam tu germani con-
strictus exemplo religionem Iudaicam deseras? Quid ergo in
5 hac terribili solitudine diutius tempus terimus? Quamdiu
etiam inopia victus laborare poterimus? praesertim cum et illi
duo iuvenes quos remisimus moram faciant, et famulis nostris
locus hic in quem devenimus penitus ignotus sit. Quo autem
fructu poenam nobis tam laboriosae mortis inferimus? Quid
10 causae est ut fame tabescamus, arescamus siti, obrigescamus
algore, et postremo, quod iam patimur, vastae huius solitudinis
horribili terreamur silentio? (14) Numquid latronum vincula,
numquid barbarorum gladios fugimus? Numquid sanguinem
nostrum plebs tam misericors quam pro nobis flere conspex-
15 imus concupiscit? Recordemur, obsecro, quem umquam
laeserit, cui nostrorum verbo saltem irrogarit iniuriam, et rever-
tamur ad innoxios, quos in nullo sensimus inimicos, et quod
Deo placuerit fiat.' (15) Ad haec Meletius, 'Ego te,' inquit,
'Innocenti frater, qui non solum Latinis verum etiam Graecis
20 litteris eruditus es et legem iugiter meditaris, oblitum reor
quod per Ezechielem prophetam Dominus ait, "Anima quae
peccaverit ipsa morietur." (16) Si enim legisti hoc, cur me fratris
mei, Theodori, exemplo adtrahi posse ad fidem Christi aestimas? Habet ille ut animam suam ita etiam et peccatum suum,
25 quod quidem mihi, si Dominum Deum patrum meorum non
reliquero, non nocebit. (17) Testor autem illum, qui eduxit
patres nostros de terra Aegypti, me, si hiemis inclementia non
obesset, abrepto qualicumque navigio ad quaslibet terras
solum velle migrare. Nec me possessionum amor nec affec-
30 tuum caritas detinet, quorum facilis mihi iactura est, tantum
ne Deum patrum nostrorum negare compellar. (18) Quod
autem consilio inutili ad civitatem remeandum decernis, miror

5 terribili *WVz*: horribili *P*    7 remisimus *PW*: praemisimus *Vz*    faciant
*PVz*: faciunt *W*    8 in quem *PW*: quo *V*: in quo *z*    9 tam *PWz*: tantam *V*
11 et postremo *PW*: ad postremum *Vz*    12 terreamur *PWVG*: terreamus *S*:
intereamus *A*: teneamur *C*    13 latronum aut *ante* barbarorum *add. P*
15 recordemur *PWVAC*: recordemus *SG*    16 irrogarit *PWVGC*: irrigavit *S*:
irrogavit *A*    17 innoxios *Vz*: nostros *PW*    19 qui *PWz*: quem *V*
20 eruditus es *Wz*: eruditus *P*: eruditum scio *V*    22 legisti *WVz*: legistis *P*
23 adtrahi *PVz*: trahi *W*    23–4 aestimas *PWz*: existimas *V*    25 peccatum *ante* mihi *add. V*    dominum *om. PW*    meorum *PWVGC*: nostrorum *SA*
26 reli(n)quero *Vz*: relinquo *PW*    27 terra *om. P*    Aegypti *WVz*: Aegypto *P*

bore witness, and I heard it with my own ears, that your brother, Theodorus, who is greater than you in learning, honour and years, converted to faith in Christ. (13) Isn't it likely that you too, constrained by the example of your own blood brother, will desert the Jewish religion? Why then should we waste time any longer in this horrible solitude? How long will we be able to struggle on, overwhelmed by a lack of provisions, especially since those two young men whom we sent back are delayed and this place to which we have come is completely unknown to our servants? For what reward, moreover, are we exposing ourselves to the punishment of so painful a death? Why should we waste away from hunger, be parched with thirst, stiffen with cold, and last of all, be terrified by the dreadful silence of this vast emptiness, which we are already suffering? (14) Are we fleeing the fetters of brigands? the swords of barbarians? Do the Christians, whom we saw weeping for our sakes, do so merciful a people desire our blood? Let us recall, I beg of you, any whom they ever harmed, any whom they so much as dealt a verbal blow. Let us return to those blameless people, whom we perceive to be in no way our enemies, and let God's will be done.' (15) Meletius said in response, 'Brother Innocentius, you are learned not only in Latin literature, but in Greek literature as well, and you meditate constantly on the Law, but I think you have forgotten what the Lord says through the prophet Ezekiel: "The soul that sinneth, it shall die" [Ezek. 18: 20]. (16) Now, if you have read this, why do you suppose that I can be drawn to faith in Christ by the example of my brother Theodorus? Just as he has his own soul, so too does he have his own sin, a sin that will not harm me if I do not abandon the Lord God of my fathers. (17) Moreover, I call to witness Him who led our fathers out of the land of Egypt that I wish to emigrate, alone, to any land whatsoever by whatever voyage possible, if only winter storms did not hinder me. Neither does love of property nor the warmth of my personal attachments hold me back, the loss of which is easy for me, provided only that I am not compelled to deny the God of my fathers. (18) But you offer the useless advice that we should return to the city. I am amazed that you, though a very wise

29 velle *om. P*     migrare *WVSGC*: migrasse *P*: navigare *A*     29–30 affectuum *PWV*: affectionum *z*     30 est *om. W*     31 nostrorum *PVz*: meorum *W*

te prudentissimum virum non animo praevidere quid de nobis futurum censeas, si Theodorus columna synagogae nostrae, in quo omnem fiduciam reponebamus, apostatare compulsus est. (19) Hoc ergo sanius est, ut eamus potius ad agrum meum nec
5 nos ultro Christianorum oculis ingeramus. Possumus autem illic interim delitescere, donec oportuno tempore ad peregrina emigremus, quoniam quidem in hac insula ita apud cunctos odium nostrae religionis increvit, ut, qui patriam non reliquerit, fidem patrum tenere non possit. Cur itaque non volun-
10 tarium suscipiamus exilium ad quod, sicut res indicat, odiis civium etiam si nolumus extrudendi sumus.' (20) Hoc igitur consilio utriusque sententia confirmata, laborem destinati itineris arripiunt. (21) Sed dum per angustissimum gradiuntur callem, cogitationum tenebris lucem excaecantibus oculorum,
15 ipsum quem inscii sequebantur tramitem perdiderunt, et in locis sentis atque inviis decidentes, cum aut scinderentur vepribus aut rupibus arcerentur. (22) Postquam corpus suum longis foedavere vulneribus, ad tantam primo quidem anxietatem deinde etiam desperationem atque formidinem venere, ut
20 compellerentur fateri se hoc iusto Dei iudicio ob incredulitatem perpeti. (23) Igitur nomen Christi, quod ante ultro se ingerens repellebant, laceratis iam cruribus invocantes, semitam quae eos contra voluntatem ac propositum suum ad oppidum retraxit corripuerunt. (24) Sed cum ad civitatem inviti
25 ac trepidi pervenissent, curiosius omnia percunctantes, audiunt Theodorum etiam nunc Iudaeum esse nec ullam, sicut aestimaverant, Christiani populi pertulisse violentiam. (25) Stupentes itaque et quod ipsis acciderat non credentes, ad domum Theodori gressus dirigunt; ubi cum eos iam paene
30 exacto prandio ille excepisset, ilico inquirit causam cur a se atque a civitate abscessissent, universumque ordinem gestae rei magis cum risu quam cum admiratione cognoscit.

---

1 te *om.* P     3 apostatare *Pz*: apostotare *V*: a potestate *W*     4 potius *PW*: tutius *Vz*     6 delitescere *WVz*: delitiscere *P*     7 emigremus *Vz*: migremus *PW*     quoniam quidem *PVA*: quamquidem *WSGC*     8–9 reliquerit *WVz*: relinquit *P*     9 patrum *PVz*: patriam *W*     tenere *PVz*: habere *W* 11 extrudendi *PWz*: extruendi *V*     12 confirmata *WV*: confirmato *Pz* 13 dum *PVz*: cum *W*     14 callem *PVz*: collem *W*     excaecantibus *PWz*: obcaecantibus *V*     15 inscii *WVz*: nescii *P*     16 cum *om.* PW 17 postquam *PV*: posteaquam *Wz*     20–1 (se) hoc iudicio ... ultro se *om.* SA: quod se ingerentes repellebantur *post* fateri *add.* A     22 laceratis *PWV*: laceris *z*

man, do not in your mind foresee what you should judge will happen to us if Theodorus, the pillar of our synagogue, in whom we placed all our trust, has been coerced into apostasy. (19) Consequently, this is the safer plan, that we go instead to my farm and not expose ourselves further to the eyes of the Christians. We can hide out there for a while until, at an appropriate moment, we can emigrate abroad, since hatred against our religion has increased to such an extent among all people on this island that whoever does not abandon his fatherland will be unable to retain his fathers' faith.[18] Why then don't we accept a voluntary exile, since the facts indicate that we are going to be driven into exile by the hatred of the citizens even if we're unwilling?' (20) With this plan they strengthened their resolve and embarked on their laborious journey. (21) But as they were making their way along a very narrow path, the darkness of their thoughts obscured the light from their eyes. They lost the path that they were following in their ignorance, and they ended up in rugged, pathless terrain, all the while scratched by brambles or obstructed by rocky outcrops. (22) Their bodies were now scarred with long cuts, and they were reduced first to such a state of anxiety, then to such a state of fearful desperation, that they were forced to confess that they were suffering this by the righteous judgement of God on account of their failure to believe. (23) Therefore, with their legs now all torn, they invoked the name of Christ, which they previously rejected when it forced itself upon them, and they took a path which led them back to town against their will and against their plan. (24) But when they had arrived at the town, reluctant and frightened, and were investigating everything rather carefully, they heard that Theodorus was still now a Jew, nor had he suffered any violence from the Christian multitude, as they had presumed. (25) Dumbfounded and not believing what had happened to them, they guided their steps toward Theodorus' house, where he received them when lunch was nearly finished, and he immediately asked them the reason why they had abandoned both him and the town. And he learned the whole narrative of events, more with a smile than with amazement.

23 suam *post* voluntatem *add. P*     26 etiam nunc *WVz*: adhuc *P*     27 aestimaverant *PWz*: existimaverant *V*     29 gressus *PW*: iter *VC, om. SAG*

**19.** Post triduum Theodorus cum contionari ad plebem suam eosque ad fidem Christi provocare disponeret, ultro se ad conversionem ingerentium Iudaeorum etiam seditionem pertulit. (2) Nemo enim ferme eorum erat qui non se palam sensisse
5 Christi potentiam contestaretur. (3) Nam primo in concilio eorum adolescens quidam, ipsius Theodori consobrinus nomine Galilaeus, ut congruis, sicut iam saepe dictum est, nominibus mysterium gestae rei usque ad finem deduceretur, cum ingenti invidia proclamare hoc coepit: (4) 'Contestor,'
10 inquit, 'vos omnes, me Iudaeum esse non posse. In possessione siquidem mea Christianos consortes habeo, quorum odiis, si in Iudaismo perseverare voluero, forsitan perimendus sum. (5) Ego igitur vitae meae periculo consulens, ad ecclesiam iam nunc pergam, ut necem quae mihi praeparatur effugiam.'
15 Haec Galilaeus cum ad tempus confingere se putaret, quasi ut causas conversionis suae reddidisse videretur, de futuri saeculi morte tunc nihil cogitans, veritatem inscius loquebatur. (6) Huic sermonem paene praeripiens, vir honestus, et non solum inter Iudaeos verum etiam in civitate usque adeo praecipuus,
20 ut etiam nunc defensor civitatis electus sit, Caecilianus vera Galilaeum dicere seque similem causam habere et similia formidare adtestabatur. (7) Quibus verbis tantam supra memorato iuveni adiecit confidentiam, ut in conspectu omnium cursu rapidissimo, quasi ad praeripiendum fidei bravium, ad
25 Galilaei nostri convolaret auxilium, et ab humilitate nostra ut eius deinceps nomine censeretur expeteret. (8) Caecilianus autem cum esset Iudaeorum pater, habito cum Floriano fratre suo aeque Iudaeorum patre maturiore consilio, huiuscemodi, sicut agnovimus, verbis synagogam adorsus est, 'Ego,' inquit,
30 'cum sim in honore synagogae post Theodorum primus, non sicut iuvenis Galilaeus cunctos quasi trepidus consulo contestorque, sed potius adhortor atque commoneo, denuntians

1 post triduum *PVAC*: post tridie *WSG*      2 Christi *om. P*      2–3 conversionem *PW*: confessionem *Vz*      3 etiam *om. V*      5 contestaretur *PVz*: protestaretur *W*      concilio *PWz*: consilio *V*      7 iam *om. W*      9 invidia *PVz*: voce *W*      proclamare *WVz*: clamare *P*      10 Iudaeum *PW*: Iudaeorum *Vz*      11 mea *PW*: in ea *Vz*      Christianos *om. SA*      13 ac *ante* periculo *add. PW* iam *om. P*      14 pergam *PVz*: pergo *W*      ut *PVGC*: *om. W*: et *SA*      ut necem quae mihi praeparatur effugiam *om. W*      17 tunc *om. W*      18 sermonem paene praeripiens *PW*: sermoni paene praeteriens *Vz*      19 Iudaeos *PVz*: suos *W* etiam *post* verum *om. W*      20 sit *WVz*: est *P*      20–1 vera Galilaeum *Vz*: vero Galilaeum vera *P*: Galilaeum vera *W*      21 et *om. Vz*      23 confidentiam

**19.** After the third day, while Theodorus was making arrangements to address the assembled people and call them to faith in Christ, he suffered a revolt from Jews who were going to offer themselves for conversion of their own accord. (2) For there was almost no one who did not testify that he had openly felt the power of Christ. (3) In fact, in their first public meeting, a certain youth, a cousin of Theodorus himself, by the name of Galilaeus (that the mystery of events, as has often been said already, may be revealed to the end with appropriate names) began to proclaim with great indignation, (4) 'I call you all to witness that I cannot be a Jew. For on my estate I have Christian partners by whose hatred I may be killed if I wish to persevere in Judaism.[19] (5) Therefore, I will heed the danger to my life and will set out right now for the church to escape the death being prepared for me.' Although Galilaeus thought he was devising these remarks for the present moment, inasmuch as he seemed to have explained the reasons for his conversion, and although he then gave no thought to the eventual end of the present age, he was unwittingly speaking the truth. (6) Caecilianus, a worthy man, and so eminent not only among the Jews but also in the town that even now he has been elected *defensor*, all but snatched Galilaeus' speech away from him, affirming that Galilaeus spoke the truth and that he himself had a similar motive and feared a similar fate. (7) With these words he instilled such great confidence in the youth that before everyone's eyes, with a quick dash, as if to carry off the prize of faith [1 Cor. 9: 24], he flew to the aid of our Galilaean [Christ], and from my own humbleness requested that henceforth he be enrolled under His name. (8) Caecilianus, however, since he was a Father of the Jews, after holding a rather hurried consultation with his brother Florianus, who was likewise a Father of the Jews,[20] addressed the synagogue, as we learned, with words of this sort, 'Since in the synagogue I am second only to Theodorus in honour, I am not advising you and making an appeal, all aflutter, as it were, like the young Galilaeus, rather I exhort you and warn you and proclaim that all of us together

ut errore pravi itineris derelicto, si fieri potest, omnes pariter ad
fidem ecclesiasticam concurramus. (9) Quod si vos ad Christum
tanta eius virtus non adtrahit, ego certe et Florianus, frater
meus, sicut recusantibus vobis tantam salutem vim inferre non
5 possumus, ita nos cum universa domo nostra religionis huius,
quam astruere non valemus, ludibria deserentes, Christianorum numero fideique sociabimur; qui numquam utique
innumerabilibus scripturarum testimoniis non solum te, frater
Theodore, qui peritior reliquis videris, sed etiam cunctos con-
10 vincerent, nisi veritatem quae vinci non potest sectarentur.' (10)
Tali Caecilianum sensu plebem suam affatum comperimus,
multosque Iudaeorum eadem die ad fidem Christi cum ipso
pariter concurrentes, cum ineffabili exultatione suscepimus.
**20.** Prodigia sane quae de caelo tunc facta sunt, cum eloqui
15 digne non valeam, silere non audeo. (2) Hora circiter septima
missam dominicam solemniter coepimus celebrare. (3) Nam
dum nos advenientes ad fidem Christi Iudaeos vel exhortamur
vel adnotamus, siquidem nomina eorum descripsimus, populus autem tanti gaudii epulis spiritualiter saginatus ut car-
20 nalium non meminisset escarum, pars diei maior effluxit. (4)
Cum igitur in ecclesia, quae paululum a civitate sequestri in
loco sita est et in qua sancti martyris Stephani nuper conditae
reliquiae conquiescunt, nobiscum pariter plebs universa
missam opperiretur, duo quidam monachi, quos Dominus
25 testes miraculorum suorum praeelegit, in campo qui ante fores
ecclesiae protenditur in herbis accubabant. (5) Vir etiam
honoratus nomine Iulius cum alio quodam de civitate ecclesiam petens, cum per ipsos praeterire coepissent, repente
unus ex monachis, viso miraculi signo conturbatus confusum
30 emisit clamorem, conversisque ad se protenta manu, quia
verbo explicare non poterat, quid videret ostendit. (6) Erat
autem globus quidam candidissimi luminis, proceritate sua
staturam quasi hominis adaequans, instar vasculorum quae

2 ecclesiasticam *PVz*: Christi *W*    4 tantam salutem *om. P*    6 deserentes *PWz*: deferentes *V*    11 sensu *PVz*: sermone *W*    affatum *P²WVz*:
allocutum *P¹*    15 valeam *PWz*: audeam *V*    18 descripsimus *PW²z*:
scripsimus *W¹V*    19 spiritualiter *om. V*    ut *om. PVz*    20 effluxit *PWz*:
effulxit *V*    22 est et *om. W*    conditae *om. W*    23 conquiescunt *PVz*:
requiescunt *W*    24 opperiretur *PWz*: aperiebatur *V*    vel expectaret *post*
opperiretur *add. W*    quidam *PWSAG*: quidem *VC*    25 praeelegit *PWVC*:
praelegit *SAG*    28 coepissent *Vz*: coepisset *PW*    28–9 repente unus *PW*

must abandon the error of our misguided way, if it can be done, and unite together in the faith of the church. (9) But even if His great power does not draw you to Christ, my brother, Florianus, and I, while we cannot use force against you in your rejection of such great salvation, none the less we, with our entire households, will abandon the mockery of this religion, which we lack the strength to defend, and we will join in alliance with the faithful ranks of the Christians. They certainly could never vanquish, with their countless citations from the Scriptures, not only you, brother Theodorus, who are thought to be more learned than the others, but everyone else as well, if they were not pursuing the truth, which cannot be defeated.' (10) With such reasoning, we learned, Caecilianus addressed his people, and on that day we received with ineffable joy many Jews who came running with him to faith in Christ.

**20.** Although I lack the ability to speak eloquently about the prodigies which occurred in the sky at that time, I do not dare to be silent. (2) At about the seventh hour, we began solemnly to celebrate the Lord's Mass. (3) The greater part of the day passed, while we were either offering encouragement to or putting on record (for we copied down their names) Jews who were arriving to confess faith in Christ, and the people were spiritually sated with such a banquet of joy that they gave no thought to earthly food. (4) The whole congregation was waiting for Mass with me in the church, which is located a short distance from the town in a secluded spot and in which repose the relics of the blessed martyr Stephen, which were recently deposited there. Meanwhile two monks, whom the Lord chose as witnesses to his miracles, were lying in the grassy field that stretched out in front of the church doors. (5) There was as well a man of rank by the name of Julius seeking the church with another man from the town. When they had started to pass by, suddenly one of the monks, distracted by the sight of a miraculous sign, uttered a garbled cry and, when they turned around toward him, pointed with an outstretched hand, since he could not describe in words what he saw. (6) There was a ball of very brilliant light, approximately the size of a man in height and

respondente uno *Vz*    30 conversisque *PVz*: conversusque *W*    protenta *PWz*: portenta *V*    quia *PWz*: quae *V*    31 quid videret *Vz*: quod viderat *P*, *om. W* 32 autem *om. V*    proceritate sua *PVz*: proceritatis suae *W*    33 quasi *om. P*

vulgo orcae appellantur. (7) Tantae vero claritatis atque ful-
goris fuit quod visum est, ut fratri qui id prior notavit, sicut ipso
referente cognovimus, sol decidere videretur. (8) Hoc sicut istis
visum est quasi trans basilicam, in qua universus nobiscum
5 populus consistebat, lento lapsu dimittebatur. (9) Verum ita id
propinquum putavere ut se idem frater stupore percitus cursu
proriperet, aestimans id post basilicam decidisse, sed ab alio
retractus fratre gressum inhibuit. (10) Ille enim ita quidem
etiam sibi visum, tamen longius fuisse, non quasi certus sed ut
10 aestimans, astruebat. (11) Mulieres autem quaedam tunc
Iudaeae, inter quas matrona Meletii illius cuius supra mentio
habita est, de cenaculo prospicientes, ita sibi id ipsum visum
esse confirmabant, quasi supra basilicam decidisset. (12)
Verum hoc, utrum angelus an ipse sanctus Stephanus an vere
15 id quod visum est fuerit, incertum etiam nunc est. (13) Eadem
sane die hora circiter quarta, id est, paulo antequam hoc
signum demonstraretur, grando minutissima, quam incolae
insulae huius gentili sermone 'argistinum' vocant, non usque-
quaque copiosa defluxit. (14) Haec, cum odor ex ea mellis
20 fragrare coepisset, a multis quos per viam verberaverat de-
gustata dulcior melle comperta est. (15) Multi itaque sapientes
cum eadem die filios Israel ab Aegypto perfidiae suae atque a
servitute egressos viderent, haec quae facta sunt signis illis,
quae in Exodo legimus, comparabant; huic populo, qui Deum
25 credulo corde intuens verum iam Israelis nomen meruit,
manna crederent renovatum. (16) Columnam quoque ignis,
quae patres in eremo praecedebat, ut etiam et filiis a vera
Aegypto atque a fornace, sicut scriptum est, ferrea egressis
ducatum praeberet ad vitam, ostensam fuisse aestimabant.
30 (17) Et re vera, sicut lectio Exodi adtestatur, similitudo signorum minime discrepabat. Nam et illud, quod nivem fuisse

1 (h)orcae *Wz*: oreae *PV*      appellantur *Pz*: dicuntur *W*: appellabantur *V*
2 fuit quod visum est ut *P*: quod visum est fuit ut *W*: ut visum fuit quod *V*: erat quod
visum fuit ut *z*      id *om. PW*      3 decidere *Vz*: decedere *PW*      5 dimittebatur *PVz*: dimittebantur *W*      6 putavere *PWVGC*: putabatur *SA*      idem
*PWz*: isdem *V*      frater *om. P*      percitus *P¹WVz*: percito *P²*      7 aestimans
*PWz*: existimans *V*      8 retractus *PWz*: retractatus *V*      gressum *Vz*: regressum
*PW*      9 etiam *om. W*      13 basilicam *WVz*: ecclesiam *P*      decidisset *PVz*:
decidissent *W*      17 demonstraretur *PWVGC*: monstraretur *S*: monstraret *A*
18 argistinum *PW*: abgistinum *Vz*      20 fragrare *edd.*: flaglare *P*: flagrare *WVG*:
fraglare *SAC*      verberaverat *WVz*: verberat *P*      21 comperta *PWVAC*: com-
parata *SG*      23 perversae dominationis *post* servitute *add. P*      esse *post* egressos

with the shape of the jugs commonly called *orcae*. (7) The vision was of such clarity and brilliance that it appeared to the brother who noticed it first, as we learned from his own account, that the sun was sinking. (8) It appeared to them to be sinking in a slow descent over the church where the entire congregation remained with me. (9) Indeed, they thought it was so close that that same brother, after being jolted out of his stupor, set out at a run, since he thought that it had sunk behind the church, but he checked his step, held back by his fellow monk. (10) The latter added that it had also appeared to him but that it was further away, though he was not positive and only guessing. (11) However, certain women who were still Jews at the time, among whom was the wife of the Meletius mentioned above, confirmed that, as they were looking out of an upper storey, the same thing appeared to them as if it had descended over the church. (12) But it is still today unclear whether this thing was an angel or St Stephen himself or what it really appeared to be. (13) At around the fourth hour on that same day, that is, slightly before this sign was revealed, there fell a light dusting of very fine hail, which the island's inhabitants in their local dialect call *argistinum*.[21] (14) After the air began to grow fragrant with the smell of honey, it was tasted by many who had been struck by it on the road and it was found to be sweeter than honey. (15) When many people tasted it and saw that on that same day the sons of Israel [viz. the Jews of Minorca] departed from the Egypt of their unbelief and from slavery, they compared what had happened to those wonders we read about in Exodus. They believed that the manna had been renewed for this people who, by their contemplation of God with a heart ready to believe, now merited the name of the true Israel [Exod. 16]. (16) They also judged that the column of fire, which preceded the Fathers in the desert, had been revealed in order to furnish spiritual guidance for the sons who had departed from the true Egypt and, as it is written, from the iron furnace [Deut. 4: 20]. (17) And in truth, as a reading of Exodus confirms, the similarity of the signs was very close. For what we believe to have been hail corresponded to the tiny coriander

*add.* P        25 iam *PWz*: etiam *V*        meruit *WVz*: promeruit *P*        26 renovatum *PW*: innovatum *Vz*        27 et *WSAG*: a *W*, *om.* PC        28 sicut *PVz*: ut
*W*        29 fuisse *WVz*: esse *P*        aestimabant *P*: aestimarent *WVz*

credimus, semen coriandri minuti adaequabat, mel sapore
referebat. Et hoc quod apparuit columnae igneae specimen
habuisse manifestum est. (18) Utrumque autem signum etiam
Iamonae consistentibus fratribus revelatum fuisse cognovimus.
5 (19) Nam et pluviam mellis multi, quibus intellectus re-
quirendi id et pergustus agnoscendi datus est, probavere, et
columna candidissimi illius luminis multorum quos dignos
Dominus iudicavit se ingessit aspectibus. (20) Unde intelligi
datur Iudaeos per universum orbem fidei lumine visitandos,
10 (21) quoniam quidem nobis qui in hac insula atque in hoc par-
vulo, ut ita dixerim, orbe consistimus, tantus caelestis gratiae
splendor illuxit, ut usque ad extremos terrae nostrae terminos
signorum visio perveniret.

**21.** Sequenti igitur die, summa omnium expectatio Theo-
15 dorum ut sponsioni suae satisfaceret admonebat, (2) qui cum
iustis, quantum ipsi videbatur, allegationibus cunctorum vota
crederet differenda, dicens matronam prius suam, quam in
Maioricensi reliquisset insula, huc se velle deducere, ne forte, si
absque consensu suo virum suum conversum fuisse agnovisset,
20 sicut solet, pertinax perfidiae esset, et persuasione matris prae-
cipue suae, quae adhuc supererat, consiliis dementata et a
coniugio et a religione discederet. (3) Cum haec Theodorus
Christianis iam acquiescentibus perorasset, Iudaeis qui con-
versi fuerant acerrima commotione consistentibus, amputata
25 dilationis mora, ad matris propinquae sinum festinus ut viderat
convolavit; (4) post quem omnis, tamquam remoto obice, ad
ecclesiam synagoga confluxit. (5) Mirum dictu, inveterati illi
legis doctores sine ulla altercatione verborum, sine ullo
scripturarum certamine crediderunt. (6) Tantum percunctati
30 an vellent fidem Christi suscipere, credere se in Christum et
Christianos statim fieri cupere profitebantur.

1 credimus *W¹Vz*: credidimus *PW²*          coriandri *PWC*: coliandri *VSAG*
1–2 mel sapore referebat *PW*: mellis saporem ferebat *Vz*      2 post *ante* apparuit
*add. PW*      specimen *PWSAG*: speciem *VC*      4 Iamonae *PWVC*: iam mane
*SAG*      fuisse *WVz*: esse *P*      6 id *om. V*      et *post* id *PVz*: est *W*      datus
*PVGC*: data *W*: datum *SA*          7 columna *PVC*: columnam *WSAG*
9 orbem *WVSC*: mundum *PAG*          15 ut *om. V*      sponsioni *PWGC*: sponsionis
*VSA*          16 quantum *PVz*: ut *W*      ipsi *PVz*: sibi *W*      videbatur *PWz*: videbantur *V*          17 dicens *om. W*          18 Maioricensi *WV²SA*: Maioricensus *P¹*,
Maioricense *P²*: Minoricensi *V¹C*: Mainoricensi *G*      deducere *PVz*: adducere *W*
19 agnovisset *WVz*: cognovisset *P*          20 esset *PWV*: esse *z*      et *om. Vz*      persuasione *Vz*: persuasionem *PW*          21–2 et a coniugio et a religione *Vz*: a coniugio
et religione *P*: a coniugio et a religione *W*          22 discederet *PVAC*: descisceret *WSG*

seed and recalled honey with its taste, and it is clear that what had appeared [in the sky over the church] was like a fiery column. (18) Moreover, we have learned that both wonders were also revealed to the brethren who remained in Jamona. (19) For many people, who had been granted the ability and disposition to enquire into this matter, attested the rain of honey, and that column of very brilliant light revealed itself to the gaze of many people whom the Lord judged worthy. (20) From which it may be inferred that Jews throughout the whole world are to be visited with the light of faith, (21) since indeed so great a splendour of heavenly grace has shone upon us, who live on this island and, if I may use the phrase, in 'this little world', so that the revelation of signs should extend to the utmost boundaries of our world.

**21.** Accordingly, on the following day, everyone reminded Theodorus with great anticipation that he should make good his pledge. (2) He believed, for what seemed to him justifiable reasons, that the vows of all the Jews should be postponed, saying that first he wanted to bring his wife here, whom he had left on the island of Majorca. His concern was that she might, if she learned that her husband had converted without her agreement, remain firm in her faithlessness, as usually happens. Further, she might become confused in her judgement and, at the instigation of her mother in particular, who was still alive, abandon both the marriage and her husband's religion. (3) When Theodorus had made these pleas, the Christians were amenable, but the Jews who had converted persisted in a bitter disturbance.[22] The delay was cut short and Theodorus himself flew swiftly to the bosom of his kinswoman, as he had seen [in the dream]. (4) After him, the whole synagogue, as if a stumbling block had been removed, flowed together to the church. (5) Marvellous to relate, aged teachers of the Law began to believe, without any verbal wrangling, without any dispute over the Scriptures. (6) After debating for so long whether they were willing to accept faith in Christ, they professed that they believed in Christ and desired to be made Christians without delay.

23 iam *om. P*   perorasset *PWz*: properasset *V*       24 co(m)motione *PWV*: com-monitione *z*   consistentibus *WVz*: insistentibus *P*       25 in somniis *ante* viderat *add. V*       26 tamquam *PWV*: quasi *z*       27 synagoga *PVSA*: synagogae *WC*, *om. G*       30 Christum *PVz*: Christo *W*

**22.** Centum quidam et duos, ut asserunt, aetatis atque perfidiae suae habens annos, sine trium commutatione verborum, spe vitae futurae alacer, decrepitus proclamavit optare se ut in fine temporum suorum per fidem Christi ad spiritualem re-
5 verteretur infantiam, nobisque putrefacta iam senio membra ut quantocius per baptismum regenerarentur ingessit.

**23.** Fuere quidam Iudaei qui, praetereuntes illuc appulsi, opportunitatem temporis atque ventorum aucupabantur; qui navigandi libertate concessa credere maluerunt.

10 **24.** Tres igitur tantummodo feminas sed nobilissimas Iudaeorum, ad virtutis suae gloriam dilatandam in duritia perfidiae suae Christus permanere aliquantulum passus est. (2) Artemisia siquidem Litorii, qui nuper hanc provinciam rexit et nunc comes esse dicitur, filia coniugis sui Meletii conversione
15 commota, cum una ferme amica et nutrice et paucis ancillulis domum viri sui deserens, ad quamdam speluncam licet in vinea tamen in remotiore paululum loco sitam, oblita femineae infirmitatis evasit. (3) Erat in ea parvum novumque torcular, lacusque nuper factus figuram quodammodo gerere credentis
20 populi videbatur. (4) Non enim istos sicut utres veteres, sed sicut novos lacus, mustum Novi Testamenti recepisse aut credimus aut videmus. (5) In eo igitur loco cum per biduum matrona a viro suo offensa inexorabilis permansisset, ut primum tertia dies illuxit, aquam ex eodem lacu, quae illic
25 ante id temporis ex pluvia confluxerat, ut faciem ex more elueret, famulae haurire imperavit. Quam cum et odore et sapore mellis dulcedinem referre sensisset, primo quidem etiam succensere ministrae coepit et cur in eodem urceo mel iniecisset indignans inquirebat. (6) Postea autem ut quasi
30 negantem convinceret ad lacum pergit, de quo paululum concavis manibus hauriens, repperit aquam de qua per biduum

1 quidam *PVSG*: quidem ~*WAC*     3 proclamavit *om. V*     in *om. W*
4 fine *PVGC*: finem *WSA*     6 quantocius *om. P*     regenerarentur *WVz*:
regenerarentur *P*     7 quidam *WVSAG*: quidem *PC*     illuc *Vz*: illic *PW*
9 libertate *om. V*     10 tantummodo *om. P*     11 dilatandam *PVz*: dilatan-
dum *W*     duritia *PWz*: duritiam *V*     12–13 Artemisia *edd.*: Artemia *PW*:
Arthemisia *V*: Art(h)imisia *SAG*: Archimisia *C*     13 Litorii *PW*: Litori *VSAG*:
Litoris *C*     14 Meletii *om. P*     15 ancillulis *PWSGC*: ancillis *VA*
16 domum *PWz*: demum *V*     sui *om. W*     17 sitam *PW*: sita *Vz*     18 ea
*WVC*: eo *PSAG*     parvum *Vz*: parum *PW*     novumque *Vz*: nudumque *PW*
19 nuper *PW*: novus *Vz*     qui *post* factus *add. W*     19–20 credentis populi *om. P*
21 novos *PWz*: novas *V*     23 a *om. PW*     suo *om. PW*     24 aquam *Vz*:

**22.** One man, so they say, was one hundred and two years in age and in faithlessness. Although decrepit, he was nimble in his hope for the future life, and without exchanging three words, he proclaimed that he hoped to return at the end of his days to a spiritual infancy through faith in Christ, and he presented to us his limbs, by now feeble with decay, that he might be renewed through baptism as quickly as possible.

**23.** There were certain Jews who, as they sailed past, were driven to the island and were waiting for an appropriate moment and favourable winds. Even though the freedom to set sail was granted them, they preferred to believe.

**24.** Consequently, only three women, although very noble women among the Jews,[23] did Christ permit to hold out a little longer, in order to extend the glory of his power amidst the hardheartedness of their unbelief. (2) Artemisia, the daughter of Litorius, who recently governed this province and who is now said to be a Count,[24] was distraught at the conversion of her husband Meletius. Without any thought for feminine frailty and with just one friend, a nurse, and a few servant girls, she deserted her husband's house and escaped to a cave, which, though located in a vineyard, was none the less in quite a remote spot. (3) In the vineyard, there was a small, new wine-press, and a newly-made vat, which seemed somehow to serve as a symbol of a faithful people. (4) For we either believe or can see that the Jews have received the 'must' of the New Testament not like 'old wineskins', but like 'new winevats' [Luke 5: 37]. (5) This woman had passed two days in that spot, implacable and angry with her husband. As soon as the third day dawned, she ordered a maidservant to draw water for her so that she could wash her face in her usual way. The water came from the winevat, which was full from a rainshower. When she realized that the water resembled honey in the sweetness of its taste and smell, at first she began to grow angry with the servant and asked indignantly why she had put honey in the pitcher. (6) Afterwards, however, as if to disprove the servant's denials, she went to the vat, drew forth a little water with cupped hands, and found that the water she had been

aqua *PW*    lacu *PW*: loco *Vz*    27 dulcedinem *PVz*: dulcedine *W*
28 succensere ministrae c(o)epit *Vz*: succensa recepit *P*: irasci in eam cepit *W*
29 postea *PWC*: postquam *VSAG*    30 pergit *WVz*: perrexit *P*    31 de *om.*
*V*    qua *PVz*: aqua *W*

usa fuerat in mellis suavissimi versam dulcedinem. (7) Ad-
vocans itaque cunctas quae aderant ut gustarent rogat, ne forte
fallax sapor in faucibus tantum ipsius suavitatem mentiretur;
(8) omnes gustantes ita mira oblectatione affectae sunt, ut non
5 aquam mellis sapore delibutam, sed mel sincerissimum solam
aquae similitudinem retinere censerent. (9) Stupore igitur per-
citae dum ad civitatem reverti parant, curiosius agentes etiam
rorem, qui in herbis plurimus erat, degustatum similem rep-
pererunt. (10) Pergens itaque ad civitatem matrona memorata
10 haec marito retulit ipsa, et per eum omnibus indicavit,
statimque ad fidem Christi sine reluctatione consensit. (11)
Verum eadem die, qua Meletii uxor amaritudinem incredulitatis abicere ex melle compulsa est, eadem, inquam, die qua
memorata filia Israel, quasi in deserto posita, illum antiquum
15 lacum Mara iniecto crucis ligno obdulcuisse persensit, ita
mirifico vereque caelesti omnis ecclesia odore fragravit, ut
praesentiam Spiritus Sancti, quam et ante iam aliquotiens sed
paucissimi senseramus, fraternitas paene universa sentiret.
**25.** Et mirum cunctis illud etiam fuit quod, per eosdem dies
20 serenitate propemodum iugiter permanente, creberrimi
imbres demittebantur. (2) Et paulatim advenientes ad fidem
Christi Iudaeos pluvia praecedebat, ita ut hoc animadvertentes
vulgo inter nos et quasi ioculariter diceremus, 'Ecce, iam pluit,
scitote quoscumque Iudaeos ad fidem Christi accessuros!'
25 Mirum dictu, frequenter, cum adhuc talia loqueremur, a quibusdam Iudaeis fidei ianua pulsabatur. (3) Nec immerito cum,
sicut scriptum est, 'Pluviam voluntariam segregans Deus
hereditati suae' crediturum populum imbres laetissimi nunti-
abant.
30 **26.** Duae adhuc supererant feminae quae in odorem un-
guentorum Christi currere recusabant: Innocentii illius, cuius
supra fecimus mentionem, matrona, cum sorore sua vener-
abili, sicut fama testis est, vidua. (2) Quae tamen ilico ut

5 delibutam *PW*: delibatam *Vz*     6 retinere *om. Vz*     7 parant *PWz*:
parantur *V*     8 plurimus *PWz*: plurimis *V*     8–9 rep(p)ererunt *PWz*:
reperierunt *V*     10 haec *Vz*: haecque *PW*     ipsa *om. V*     12 die *om. VSGC*
13 qua *om. W*     15 lacum Mara *P*: merere lacum *W*: lacum myrrae *Vz*     obdulcuisse *PW*: obdulcasse *Vz*     18 iam *ante* paene *add. P*     19 et *om. PW*
20 serenitate *PW*: serena *Vz*     21 demittebantur *WVC*: dimittebantur *PSAG*
advenientes *PW*: venientes *Vz*     ad *PWSA*: in *VGC*     25 cum *P*: dum *WVz*
27 sicut *om. PA*     Deus *Pz*: Dominus *V*, *om. W*     28 hereditati suae *om. PW*

using for two days was changed into the sweetest, most delightful honey. (7) Then she called over all the women present and told them to taste the water, lest by chance a falsely sweet taste was deceiving her throat alone. (8) All of them tasted it and were stirred with such marvellous delight that they decided it was not water infused with honey, but the purest honey with only a resemblance to water. (9) Struck with wonder, they investigated more carefully while they were preparing to return to town and discovered that the dew, which was on much of the grass, also had a similar taste. (10) Accordingly, the previously mentioned lady set out for the town, reported these things to her husband, and through him made them known to everyone, and immediately, without resistance, she assented to faith in Christ. (11) However, on the same day when Meletius' wife was compelled by the honey to cast away the bitterness of her unbelief, on the same day, I say, when this daughter of Israel was placed as if in a desert, and perceived that ancient lake of Marah grow sweet when the 'log of the cross' was thrown into it [Exod. 15: 23–5], the entire church grew fragrant with such a marvellous and truly heavenly odour that nearly all the brethren sensed the presence of the Holy Spirit, which we had also sensed sometimes in the past, but only a few of us.

25. It was also counted a marvel in everyone's mind that, although the sky was for the most part clear during those days, quite frequent showers did occur. (2) And the rain would precede by a short interval Jews who were coming to confess faith in Christ. We actually noticed it and would say to one another half-jokingly, 'Look, it's raining now. Mark my words, some Jews are sure to accept faith in Christ!' Miraculously, often while we were saying such things, there would be a knock on the church door by some Jews. (3) And not in vain did those most joyful showers announce that a people would believe, since, as it is written, 'The Lord sets apart a plentiful rain for his inheritance' [Ps. 67: 10].

26. There still remained two women who refused to race to the fragrance of Christ's unguents: the wife of that Innocentius whom we mentioned above, along with her sister, a widow of excellent reputation. (2) Yet the moment she learned that her

30 duae adhuc (super)erant *PWz*: desuper erant *V*    odorem *PWSAG*: odore *VC*
33 est *om. W*

Innocentium sororis coniugem conversum esse conspexit, navem ascendit, non solum permittentibus verum etiam suadentibus nobis, quia ad fidem Christi nec verbis nec miraculis flecteretur.

5 **27.** Uxor vero Innocentii per quattuor ferme dies verbum salutis quod ingerebamus obduratis auribus reiciebat. (2) Haec cum omnem respuens medicinam insanabili incredulitatis valetudine opprimeretur, (3) nullisque Innocentii coniugis vel minis vel precibus vel lacrimis moveri posset, universa Inno-
10 centio rogante ad domum in qua habitabat fraternitatis multitudo convenit, habens magnum dolorem animi quod tantae laetitiae plenitudini una mulier obsisteret, quia iam soror eiusdem navigasse putabatur. (4) Cum igitur diu cassa verba surdis auribus ingerentes nihil profecissemus, ad cognitum
15 orationis praesidium convolavimus precesque, quas humana repellebat impietas, ad caelestem misericordiam vertimus. (5) Itaque usque in horam ferme tertiam, hymnorum atque orationum proeliis adversus Amalech hostem Iesu ducis nostri sudavit exercitus. (6) Inde cum iam paene, quod fatendum est,
20 desperantes abscessionem moliremur, resumptis rursum viribus, orationem cunctis indiximus, soloque prostrati diu flevimus. (7) Et cum in consummatione orationis 'Amen' populus inclamasset, illa credere et se Christianam fieri velle subiunxit. Nos itaque etiam hac a diaboli laqueis eruta laeti, ad
25 habitacula nostra perreximus.

**28.** Sequenti igitur id est octava demum postquam veneramus die, Iamonam remeare statuimus opima praeclarae victoriae gaudiorum spolia reportantes. (2) Sed cum iam in procinctu itineris constituti civitate digrederemur, Dominus populo suo
30 quasi pro viatico gaudium quod solum deesse videbatur adiecit. (3) Affinis siquidem Innocentii illa vidua de pelago reducta est; (4) quae subito meis se genibus advolvens, fidei nostrae auxilium cum lacrimis deprecabatur. (5) Cui ego,

1 suae *post* sororis *add.* P     conspexit *PVz*: aspexit *W*     2 ascendit *PW*: conscendit *Vz*     3 nobis *om. PW*     quia *PVz*: qui *W*     6 reiciebat *PW*: recipiebat *Vz*     10 qua *WVz*: quo *P*     12 obsisteret *WVz*: obstitisset *P*     14 auribus *om. W*     15 praesidium *WVz*: studium *P*     16 vertimus *WVz*: convertimus *P*     17 usque *om. P*     atque *PW*: et *Vz*     18 populi Dei *post* hostem *add. P*     20 moliremur *WVz*: moliremus *P*     21 diu *post* soloque *add. P*     23 amen *post* inclamasset *add. W*     24 eruta *PWz*: erupta *V*     26 igitur *om. Wz*     octava demum postquam veneramus die *P*: qua veneramus octava

sister's husband, Innocentius, had been converted, she boarded ship. We not only permitted her to do this, we even encouraged her, because she could not be turned to faith in Christ by either words or miracles.

**27.** Moreover, Innocentius' wife for nearly four days rejected with deaf ears the word of salvation that we were administering. (2) Since she was overwhelmed by the incurable sickness of her unbelief and refused all our medicine, (3) and could not be swayed by Innocentius' threats nor his prayers nor his tears, the whole crowd of the brethren, at Innocentius' request, gathered together at the house where he lived, feeling great pain in their spirits because so great an abundance of happiness was being opposed by a single woman (since her sister was thought already to have set sail). (4) After we had forced vain words on deaf ears for a long time and had accomplished nothing, we hastened to the known assistance of prayer and turned toward heavenly mercy the prayers which mortal impiety rejected. (5) And so our army sweated until nearly the third hour in contests of hymns and prayers against Amalec, the enemy of our leader Jesus [Exod. 17: 8–17]. (6) When we had become (it must be confessed) nearly desperate and were preparing our departure, we ordered everyone to regather their strength and to pray. Stretched out on the floor, we wept for a long time. (7) And when the people had exclaimed 'Amen' at the end of the prayer, that woman added that she believed and that she wanted to be made a Christian. Thereupon, we returned to our houses, delighted that this woman too had been freed from the snares of the devil.

**28.** On the following day, that is, the eighth day after we had come, we decided to return to Jamona, carrying back the rich spoils of our joy from our splendid victory. (2) But when we had made ourselves ready and were already leaving the city, the Lord added for his people as a kind of travelling allowance the one joy that appeared to be lacking. (3) For that widowed kinswoman of Innocentius was carried back from the open sea. (4) Suddenly, she wrapped herself about my knees and begged with tears for the assistance of our faith. (5) 'Why woman', I

demum die *W*: octava demum qua die veneramus *Vz*      27 Iamonam *z*: Iamona *PV*: iam nona *W*      28 iam *om. W*      30 solum deesse *om. P*      32 reducta *WVz*: adducta *P*      33 deprecabatur *WVz*: precabatur *P*

'Cur,' inquam, 'mulier, tanta animi levitate fratres tuos deserere voluisti?' Ad haec illa, 'Et Ionas', inquit, 'propheta a facie Domini fugere voluit, et tamen voluntatem Domini licet invitus implevit. (6) Suscipe ergo et tu non solum me verum
5 etiam et istas orphanas, et Christo eas nutri.' (7) Et hoc miserabiliter inclamans, duas filias suas parvulas mihi cum fletibus ingerebat. (8) Quis non prae gaudio flevit? Cui non extorsit lacrimas laetitiae magnitudo? (9) Suscepi plane ovem quam ex omni numero solam errasse putabamus, eamque
10 cum gemino foetu ad Christi ovilia revocavi.

**29.** Sane per hos octo quibus haec omnia gesta sunt dies, ante initium quadragesimae quasi paschae a nobis est celebrata festivitas. (2) Quingentas siquidem et quadraginta animas ad ecclesiam constat adiectas. (3) Inane autem et supervacuum
15 non reor ut, cum multa propter infinitam copiam praetermisero, in fine commemorem neminem ex tanta Iamonensis populi multitudine, praesertim quae per triginta milia passuum ante tot dies venerat, aut curam domus suae aut provisionem substantiae aut desiderium affectuum huic operi
20 praetulisse.

**30.** Illud magis mirum magisque gaudendum est, quod ipsam Iudaicae plebis terram diu inertem, nunc autem recissis incredulitatis vepribus et recepto verbi semine, multiplicem fructum iustitiae germinare conspicimus, ita ut nobis in spe
25 tantorum novalium gaudeamus. (2) Nam unde insignem perfidiae eruimus silvam, illic laetissima fidei opera pullularunt. Primum enim ipsa synagogae fundamenta vertere, deinde ad novam basilicam construendam non solum impendia conferunt, sed etiam humeris saxa comportant.

30 **31.** Haec Beatitudo vestra die quarto nonarum februariarum virtute Domini nostri Iesu Christi arrepta octo diebus ab eodem consummata esse cognoscat, post consulatum Domini Honorii undecimum et Constantii iterum viri clarissimi.

2 Ionas *PW*: Iona *Vz*        propheta *om. W*        3 Domini *PW*: Dei *Vz*
4 verum *PVz*: sed *W*        5 et *ante* istas *om. W*        eas *PVz*: illas *W*        6 parvulas
*om. P*        9 errasse *Vz*: deesse *P*: deerrasse *W*        10 ovilia *PVz*: ovile *W*
12 quasi *om. Vz*        13 et *om. Vz*        14 et *PVz*: ac *W*        15 non *om. PW*
cum *WVz*: qui *P*        16 fine *PVz*: finem *W*        17 praesertim *om. V*        quae
*PWz*: qui *V*        19 desiderium affectuum *PW*: desiderii affectum *Vz*
24 nobis *PWV*: nos *z*        25 nam *om. Vz*        26 fidei opera *om. z*
28 impendia *PVz*: impensa *W*        29 in *ante* humeris *add. P*        saxa *om. P*
30 quarto *Vz*: tertio *PW*        februariarum *PVSA*: februarium *WG*

asked, 'did you wish to desert your brothers in such foolhardiness?' To which she replied, 'Even the prophet Jonah wished to flee from the countenance of God, and yet he fulfilled, although unwillingly, the will of God [Jonah 1: 1–4]. (6) Therefore, receive not just myself, but these orphans too, and nourish them in Christ.' (7) While she was making this pitiful plea, she led her two little daughters to me. (8) Who did not weep for joy? From whom did this abundance of happiness not wring tears? (9) To be sure, I accepted the sheep (the only one from the whole flock we knew to have wandered off) and I recalled her with her twin offspring to the fold of Christ.

**29.** Although the eight days in which these events occurred were before the beginning of Lent, they were celebrated by us as if it were Easter. (2) For it is confirmed that 540 souls were added to the church. (3) Moreover, I do not think it frivolous or superfluous (though I will have omitted many things due to my endless supply) to recollect in closing that of the great multitude of people from Jamona who had come so many days before on a journey of thirty miles, not one placed concern for his house, or plans for his daily sustenance, or personal affections before this task.

**30.** All the more joy should be felt at the following marvel, namely that we see the land of the Jewish people, barren for so long, producing manifold fruits of righteousness, now that the thorns of unbelief have been cut down and the seed of the Word implanted, so that we rejoice for ourselves in the hope of new crops. (2) Where we uprooted an infamous forest of unbelief, the most fertile works of faith have flourished. For not only are the Jews bearing the expense, first, for levelling the very foundations of the synagogue, and then, for constructing a new basilica, but they even carry the stones on their own shoulders.[25]

**31.** May your Blessedness know that these things were begun on the fourth day before the Nones of February by the power of our Lord Jesus Christ and were completed on the eighth day hence,[26] in the year after the eleventh consulship of the Emperor Honorius and the second consulship of Constantius,

31 arrepta *PVG*: incepta *W*: arrecta *SA*    32 cognoscat *PVz*: cognoscit *W* 32–3 Domini *om. PW*    33 Constantii *PW*: Constantio *Vz*    iterum *om. P*    viri clarissimi *PW*: victoriae *V*: victore *z*

(2) Quamobrem si indigni et peccatoris verbum dignanter admittitis, zelum Christi adversum Iudaeos sed pro eorumdem perpetua salute suscipite. (3) Forsitan enim iam illud praedictum ab Apostolo venit tempus, ut plenitudine gentium
5 ingressa omnis Israel salvus fiat. (4) Et fortasse hanc ab extremo terrae scintillam voluit Dominus excitari, ut universus orbis terrarum caritatis flagraret incendio ad exurendam infidelitatis silvam.

1 et *om.* W    2–3 pro eorumdem perpetua salute *PW*: propter Deum eorumdem perpetuam salutem *V*: propter eorumdem perpetuam salutem *z*    3 suscipite *Pz*: suscipere *WV*    5 ingressa *WVz*: introgressa *P*    extremo *PWz*: extrema *V*

## CHAPTER 31

a man of *clarissimus* rank.[27] (2) Wherefore, if you accept respect-
fully the word of an unworthy sinner, take up Christ's zeal
against the Jews, but do so for the sake of their eternal salvation. (3) Perhaps that time predicted by the Apostle has indeed
now come when the fullness of the Gentiles will have come in
and all Israel shall be saved [Rom. 11: 25–6]. (4) And perhaps
the Lord wished to kindle this spark from the ends of the earth,
so that the whole breadth of the earth might be ablaze with the
flame of love in order to burn down the forest of unbelief.

6 excitari *WVz*: excitare *P*      7 flagraret *Wz*: fraglaret *P*: flagret *V*      7–8 ad
exurendam infidelitatis silvam *om. WVz*      8 explicit *add. W*      explicit epistola
Severi episcopi *add. VS*

# NOTES

1. Ancient geographers confirm Severus' remarks about the peculiarities of Minorca's fauna. Strabo 3. 5. 2 (168) comments on the absence of harmful beasts in the Balearics; Pliny *Hist. Nat.* 35. 202 confirms that snakes did not prosper there. For further references to the topography and wildlife of the Balearics, see W. Smith, *A Dictionary of Greek and Roman Geography* (London, 1873) *s.v.* Baleares.
2. Severus is consistent in his claim that the entire Jewish community of Minorca lives in the eastern town, Magona, with its better harbour. Evidence for Jewish communities tends to cluster in places that were on trade routes, either because many Jews were involved in commerce as traders or artisans, or because as immigrants they tended to settle in places that were more open to outside influences; see Cracco Ruggini, 'Ebrei e orientali' 204, 216.
3. This priest was Paulus Orosius. On the discovery of the relics and Orosius' travels, see Introduction, section iv.
4. Stephen's love working through his relics kindles the ardour of the Christians, but the saint, surprisingly in a hagiographical text, plays only a very minor role in events (cf. 6. 4; 20. 4, 12). Orosius' deposition of the relics in the church at Magona was a surprisingly informal affair. No *adventus* ceremony is mentioned, nor does Severus appear strongly interested in the elaboration of Stephen's cult. Christ's power (*virtus*), not the saint's, determines the course of events. See Introduction pp. 43–4, 63–5.
5. These lines attest the previously amicable relations between Christians and Jews on Minorca. Not only were greetings customary (*salutationis officia*), but friendships and warm feelings were common (*consuetudo familiaritatis* and *noxia inveteratae species caritatis*). Relations between the two communities have now been ruptured. Cf. Venant. Fortun. *Vita S. Hilarii* 3 (*MGH AA* 4. 2, p. 2) for the scrupulous piety of St Hilary, who achieved what Fortunatus conceded to be difficult for most people, that is, he refrained from dining with or even exchanging greetings with heretics and Jews. Note also the the reaction of Christians to Theodorus' agreement to convert at 16. 18.
6. *Pater pateron*: on Minorca's gentry and their titles, see Introduction pp. 30–4, 38.
7. Severus draws an explicit contrast between two kinds of *patrocinium*: the conventional, worldly, and, from a Christian point of view, problematical patronage of a Jewish notable vs. the superior, 'clean' power of the saint. For an analysis of the events on Minorca in terms of 'tainted' and 'clean' power, see Brown, *Cult of the Saints* 103–5.

8. This *commonitorium* does not survive, unless Seguí Vidal, *La carta-encíclica*, 67–72 is correct in identifying the *de altercatione ecclesiae et synagogae dialogus* once attributed to Augustine (*PL* 42. 1131–41) as Severus' *commonitorium*. Such *altercationes* were quite common, but failed to win converts. Gregory of Tours' frustration is no doubt typical of such encounters: 'Despite all my arguments, this wretched Jew felt no remorse and showed no sign of believing me' (*Hist. Franc.* 6. 5, *MGH SRM* 1. 249). On the failure of debate, see Blumenkranz, *Juifs et chrétiens* 68–75. On the *commonitorium*, see Seguí Vidal and Hillgarth, *La 'Altercatio'*; Demougeot, 'L'Évêque Sévère', 24–34. On anti-Jewish polemic, see A. Lukyn Williams, *Adversus Iudaeos* (Cambridge, 1935); Simon, *Verus Israel*, 135–78.

9. The synagogue is often portrayed as a widow, sometimes a rich widow, cf. *De altercat. eccl. et syn. dial.* (*PL* 42. 1131, 1135); Jer. *Comm. on Ezek.* 13. 44 (*CCL* 75. 664): *vidua et repudiata est synagoga, id est congregatio Iudaeorum, quae dominum non recepit.*

10. Theodorus' dream will come to pass, since a certain Reuben will be the first-born of them all, that is, the first Jew to convert, just as Reuben was the first-born of Jacob (*primogenitus Ruben* [Gen. 35: 23]). He will play a key role in the narrative in persuading Theodorus to convert (cf. 16. 12–16). The kinswoman who receives Theodorus to her bosom symbolizes the church. The text adduced by Severus, *una est propinqua mea*, is not in the Vulgate but recalls Song of Songs 6: 8: *una est columba mea perfecta mea.* The *propinqua* will be mentioned twice more, at 16. 19 and 21. 3.

11. The trip from Jamona to Magona took place, according to 31. 1, on 2 Feb. 418. Severus appears to be compressing the duration of the trip at 12. 2, since it is unlikely that the Christians of Jamona marched thirty miles to Magona, engaged in a street riot, burned down the synagogue, and attended a church service, all in the space of one day.

12. Severus' self-confidence and high-handedness are nowhere more conspicuous than in this chapter. He characterizes the Jews' refusal to meet with him as an 'unexpected message' (*inopinatum nuntium*), but it is unclear whether the Jews are backing out of an agreement out of fear (cf. 6. 4) or whether Severus has simply appeared unannounced and is demanding a debate. The Jews rely on a long-standing law, renewed in 412 by Honorius and Theodosius, affirming that Jews cannot be compelled to engage in public or private business (*negotium publicum vel privatum*) on the Sabbath, cf. *CTh* 16. 8. 20. Severus attempts to shift the debate to a 'common-sense' interpretation of the Old Testament, pointing out that no one is asking them to do 'menial labour' (*opus servile*). Note the sarcastic challenge that they point to the prohibition on 'engaging in discussion' (*sermonem conferre*) on the Sabbath.

13. 'Terror of that Lion', that is, the power of Christ, drives the Jews to meet with Severus. This appeal to the supernatural discreetly masks the more mundane combination of persuasion and threats applied by the bishop. When Severus has the leaders of the Jews in his presence, he shows no interest in debate. Instead he accuses the Jews of plotting violence within the town. The irony for the Jews as the weaker party is that in gathering weapons for self-defence (if Severus' accusations are true), they have left

themselves open to the accusation that they are engaged in an illegal resort to force. The only secular authorities mentioned in the letter are the *defensor*, Caecilianus, and the *patronus municipum*, Theodorus, and it appears that in Feb. 418 the secular authorities were predominantly Jews. The natural mediator in such a situation would be the *patronus*, but Theodorus is in no position to mediate. No mention is made of an attempt to secure the intervention of the provincial governor, who undoubtedly resided on Majorca. In any event, no secular authorities step in to lessen tensions between the two religious communities. Severus usurps their authority and in effect accuses the Jews of plotting sedition and violence within the town. The Jews readily deny this accusation on oath, but Severus will, in his view, clinch the argument and thereby justify any acts of physical coercion by uncovering the weapons hidden within the synagogue.

14. Psalm 9: 7–8. No detail in the letter reveals so clearly the intimacy of the two religious communities as the fact that they can sing the same hymns. In 393 local Jews assisted Ambrose and his congregation in the disinterment of Saints Vitalis and Agricola, who had been buried in a Jewish cemetery. As the holy relics were lifted from the ground, Jews and Christians chanted biblical passages responsively to one another, cf. Ambr. *Exhort. Virg.* 7–8 (*PL* 16. 353). Jews sometimes attended Christian masses and participated with Christians in certain ceremonial occasions, particularly at the funerals of well–loved bishops, including Ambrose, cf. Paulinus, *Vita Ambr.* 48 (*PL* 14. 46). For further references, see Blumenkranz, *Juifs et chrétiens* 42–3, 85–8. These examples lend some credence to claims made in the *Acta Sanctorum*, for example, that the life of 'Venantius of Arles was so beautiful that he was loved alike by Hebrews, Greeks, and Jews' (*AASS*, 30 May), or the claim that Agatha of Catania was so well loved that 'Jews and Gentiles as well as Christians revered her grave' (*AASS*, 1 Feb.). Tradition affirmed that some Christian martyrs had been buried in Jewish cemeteries, e.g. Agricola and Vitalis at Milan (*AASS*, 4 Nov.), Hermes, Aggaeus and Gaius in Dacia (*AASS*, 4 Jan.), and Vincent and Orantius in Spain (*AASS*, 22 Jan.).

15. On greed as a motive in religious coercion, note the comment of Caesarius of Arles to an imaginary opponent, '*Et tamen hic forte adhuc respondebis: Ego non ex aliquo odio poenam ingero, des de dilectione potius disciplinam; ideo expolio Iudaeum, ut per hanc asperam et salubrem disciplinam faciam christianam*' (*Sermo* 183. 6, *CCL* 104. 748).

16. On the rash of synagogue burnings in the late 4th and early 5th cents., see Introduction pp. 53–5. We learn nothing about Minorca's synagogue, but much work has been done recently on diaspora synagogues, cf. A. T. Kraabel, 'The Diaspora Synagogue: Archaeological and Epigraphic Evidence since Sukenik', in *ANRW* 19 (1979), 477–510; J. Gutmann (ed.), *Ancient Synagogues: The State of Research* (Brown Judaic Studies, 22; Chico, Calif., 1981); L. I. Levine, *Ancient Synagogues Revealed* (Detroit, 1982); id. (ed.), *The Synagogue in Late Antiquity* (Philadelphia, 1987).

17. Innocentius had fled the fighting that had begun on the mainland in late Sept. 409 and had continued intermittently until winter 417/18 (see Intro-

duction, p. 49–51). Minorca would be spared invasion until 425, cf. Hydatius, *Chron.* 86 (*s.a.* 425): *Vandali Baliaricas insulas depraedantur*.

18. *qui patriam non reliquerit, fidem patrum tenere non possit*: At Clermont-Ferrand in 576, Bishop Avitus, after failing to convert the Jews by persuasion and after the synagogue was burned to the ground, gave them a choice between baptism and exile. At the request of Gregory of Tours, Venantius Fortunatus composed a poem on the events in which Avitus offers a clear choice to the Jews: *aut admitte preces aut, rogo, cede loco.* | *vis hic nulla premit, quo vis te collige liber:* | *aut meus esto sequax aut tuus ito fugax.* | *redde, colone, locum, tua duc contagia tecum:* | *aut ea sit sedes, si tenet una fides* (Venan. Fortun. *Carm.* 5. 5. 66–70, *MGH AA* 4. 1, p. 110). Many Jews accepted baptism, but others escaped to Marseilles (Gregory of Tours, *Hist. Franc.* 5. 11, *MGH SRM* 1. 200–1). For similar episodes, particularly in Spain in the 7th cent., see Blumenkranz, *Juifs et chrétiens* 99–134.

19. The *Theodosian Code* preserves many rulings on the rights and duties of partners or coparties (*consortes*) who own land in common, cf. *CTh* 2. 5. 1 (Constantinian); 2. 5. 2 (362); 3. 1. 6 (391); 5. 16. 34 (425); 8. 18. 7 (395); 10. 14. 1 (315); 11. 22. 2 (385).

20. Although their precise functions are unknown, *pater/mater synagogae* are well-attested terms for synagogue officials, e.g. *CTh* 16. 8. 4 (331); *CIJ* i² 509 (Παγχάριος πατὴρ συναγωγῆς Ἐλαίας). Cf. Juster, *Les juifs*, i. 440–1, 448–9; Brooten, *Women Leaders* 57–72. The shortened titles *pater* and *mater* are also well-attested, e.g. *JIWE* i 1 (= *CIJ* i² 646), 56 (*CIJ* i² 612), 116 (= *CIJ* i² 619d); 63 (*CIJ* i² 606) attests a feminine *pateressa*. Severus' *pater Iudaeorum* is clearly a synonym, cf. *CIJ* i² 510: πατρὸς συναγωγῆς Αἰβρέων (= Ἐβραίων).

21. The MSS report both *argistinum* and *abgistinum*. In either case, the word is unattested elsewhere.

22. Apostates had a stake in the conversion of the entire community. The perseverance of part of the community in the old customs would be not only a psychological strain and disruptive to social relations, but it might be dangerous as well for both parties. The deterioration in Jewish–Christian relations that led to the synagogue burning in Clermont-Ferrand in 576 began when an angry Jew dumped rancid oil on the head of a recent convert as he paraded white-robed from the church after the baptismal ceremony (Gregory of Tours, *Hist. Franc.* 5. 11, *MGH SRM* 1. 200). In 582 King Chilperic ordered Jews to convert and with his own hands even helped some of them from the baptismal pool. But the order, as we might expect, was not strictly enforced and it was apparently an open secret that Jews continued to meet for services. While on his way to one of these semi-clandestine synagogue meetings, a prominent Jew called Priscus was assassinated by a recent convert to Christianity. Although pardoned by the king, the new convert was soon dispatched by Priscus' relatives, cf. Gregory of Tours, *Hist. Franc.* 6. 17, *MGH SRM* 1. 260, with W. Goffart, 'The Conversions of Avitus of Clermont, and Similar Passages in Gregory of Tours', in Neusner and Frerichs, *'To See Ourselves as Others See Us'*, 473–97; B. Brennan, 'The Conversion of the Jews of Clermont in AD 576', *JThS* 36 (1985), 321–35.

23. The last chapters of the letter concern the obstinate refusal of a few noble

Jewish women to convert. Severus has described the process by which several prominent men, Theodorus, Caecilianus, Meletius, and Innocentius, came to accept conversion to Christianity. In the final chapters of the letter, he recounts the conversion process of the wives of Meletius and Innocentius, and of Innocentius' sister-in-law, all of whom held out longer against Severus than their menfolk. Meletius and Innocentius had considered exile, but had lost heart. Only the sister-in-law of Innocentius actually boarded ship and hazarded a Feb. sea-crossing, only to return and beg forgiveness from the triumphant bishop (26. 2, 28. 3–9). We have already seen that Theodorus feared that his wife would divorce him if he acted without consulting her (21. 2). The independence and courage of these women in the face of Christian intimidation are very conspicuous, but it is unclear why they were less susceptible to the application of terror than their male kin. On Jewish women in this period, see Brooten, *Women Leaders*, *passim*; R. S. Kraemer, 'A New Inscription from Malta and the Question of Women Elders in the Diaspora Jewish Communities', *HTR* 78 (1985), 431–38; ead., 'Jewish Women in the Diaspora World of Late Antiquity', in J. R. Baskin (ed.), *Jewish Women in Historical Perspective* (Detroit, 1991), 43–67; and most recently, ead., *Her Share of the Blessings: Women's Religions Among Pagans, Jews, and Christians in the Greco-Roman World* (New York and Oxford, 1992).

24. On Litorius, see Introduction, pp. 34–7.

25. In cases of synagogue burning in the late 4th and early 5th cents., the issue of compensation was hotly disputed. It was common for the bishop to consecrate the site of the synagogue so that it could never again be returned to the Jews, cf. *CTh* 16. 8. 25 (423). The details of ch. 31 reveal how tough Severus has been in negotiations with Theodorus and other Jewish notables. Conversion was only part of the bargain. They have been compelled to provide both the money and the labourers to build a new Christian basilica on the site of the old synagogue.

26. *Haec Beatitudo vestra die quarto nonarum februariarum virtute Domini nostri Iesu Christi arrepta octo diebus ab eodem consummata esse cognoscat, post consulatum Domini Honorii undecimum et Constantii iterum viri clarissimi.* Severus' chronological specificity is striking and I am inclined to accept the claim that the events of the letter transpired from 2–9 Feb. Hunt, 'St Stephen in Minorca' 107 suggests that Severus' chronological precision is more apparent than real. On Hunt's view, the eight-day duration of the episode is 'hardly fortuitous', since the liturgical octave was 'integral to the celebration of the church's festivals'. But it is not Severus' manner to hint so obliquely at the meaning of events. If he were attaching some special importance to the number 8, he would say so, as he does in the case of the names of Reuben and Galilaeus (cf. 15. 1; 19. 3). On the significance of the number 8, see A. Quacquarelli, *L'ogdoade patristica e suoi reflessi nella liturgia e nei monumenti* (Bari, 1973).

27. Scholars have sometimes hesitated about the year (417 or 418), but 418 is clearly the correct date. The phrase *post consulatum* plus genitive is common from the late 4th to the 6th cents., apparently because the dissemination of the consuls' names was often so delayed that the present consuls might be

NOTES

unknown until well into the year. The consuls of the previous year were more easily known. Cf. *CIL* 9. 6192: *pos(t) consulatum d(omini) n(ostri) Arcadi Aug(usti) et Flavi Rufini v(irorum) c(larissimorum) con(sulum)* = AD 393; 9. 259: *post con(sulatum) d(ominorum) n(ostrorum) Arcadi III et Onori II Aug(ustorum)* = AD 395; 9. 1365: *post cons(ulatum) Honori VIII et Theodosi III Aug(ustorum)* = AD 411. On postconsular dating, see Introduction p. 4.

# BIBLIOGRAPHY

PRIMARY SOURCES

AUGUSTINE, *La Cité de Dieu XIX–XXII*, ed. G. Coulée (Bibliothèque augustinienne, 37; Paris, 1960).
—— *De Civitate Dei*, ed. E. Hoffmann (*CSEL* 40(1), Vienna, 1899; 40(2), Vienna, 1900).
—— *Epistolae ex duobus codicibus nuper in lucem prolatae*, ed. J. Divjak (*CSEL* 88; Vienna, 1981).
—— *Epistulae*, ed. Al. Goldbacher (*CSEL* 44, Vienna, 1904; 57, Vienna, 1911).
—— *De Excidio Urbis Romae Sermo*, ed. S. M. V. O'Reilly (Patristic Studies, 89; Washington, D. C., 1955).
—— *Letters: Volume VI (1\*–29\*)*, ed. R. B. Eno (The Fathers of the Church, 81; Washington, D.C., 1989).
—— *Œuvres de Saint Augustin*, ed. J. Divjak (Bibliothèque augustinienne, 46B; Paris, 1987).
HYDATIUS, *Chronique*, ed. A. Tranoy (Sources chrétiennes, 218–19; Paris, 1974).
OROSIUS, *Historiarum adversum Paganos Libri VII*, ed. C. Zangemeister (*CSEL* 5; Vienna, 1882).


SECONDARY SOURCES

ALTANER, B., 'Avitus von Braga', *ZKG* 60 (1941), 456–68.
AMENGUAL I BATLE, J., 'Noves fonts per a la historia de les Balears dins el Baix Imperi', *Bolleti de la Societat Arqueològica Lulliana*, 37 (1979), 99–111.
—— 'Informacions sobre el priscillianisme a la Tarraconense segons l'Ep. 11 de Consenci', *Instituto de Arqueologia y Prehistoria, Universidad de Barcelona*, 15–16 (1979–80), 319–38.
—— 'L'església de Tarragona al començant del segle V, segons la correspondència de Consentius a sant Agustí', *Randa*, 16 (1984), 5–17.

—— (ed.), *Correspondència amb Sant Agustí*, i (Barcelona, 1987).

—— *Els orígens del cristianisme a les Balears i el seu desenvolupament fins a l'època musulmana*, 2 vols. (Majorca, 1991–2).

APPLEBAUM, S., 'The Legal Status of the Jewish Communities in the Diaspora', in S. Safrai and M. Stern (edd.), *The Jewish People in the First Century*, i (Compendia Rerum Iudaicarum ad Novum Testamentum; Philadelphia, 1974), 420–63.

—— 'The Organization of the Jewish Communities in the Diaspora', in S. Safrai and M. Stern (edd.), *The Jewish People in the First Century*, i (Compendia Rerum Iudaicarum ad Novum Testamentum; Philadelphia, 1974), 464–503.

ARCHER, L. J., 'The Role of Jewish Women in the Religion, Ritual and Cult of Graeco-Roman Palestine', in A. Cameron and A. Kuhrt (edd.), *Images of Women in Antiquity* (London, 1983), 273–87.

—— *Her Price is Beyond Rubies: The Jewish Woman in Graeco-Roman Palestine* (Journal for the Study of the Old Testament, 60; Sheffield, 1990).

AZIZA, C., 'Juifs et judaïsme dans le monde romain: État des recherches (1976–1980)', *Revue des études latines*, 59 (1981), 44–52.

BACHRACH, B. S., *Early Medieval Jewish Policy in Western Europe* (Minneapolis, 1977).

—— 'The Jewish Community of the Later Roman Empire as seen in the *Codex Theodosianus*', in J. Neusner and E. S. Frerichs (edd.), '*To See Ourselves as Others See Us*': *Christians, Jews, and 'Others' in Late Antiquity* (Chico, Calif., 1985), 399–421.

BAER, Y., *A History of the Jews in Christian Spain* (Philadelphia, 1961).

—— 'Israel, the Christian Church and the Roman Empire from the Time of Septimius Severus to the Edict of Toleration of AD 313', in A. Fuks and I. Halpern (edd.), *Scripta Hierosolymitana*, vii (Jerusalem, 1961), 79–149.

BAGNALL, R. S., CAMERON, A., SCHWARTZ, S. R. *et al.* (edd.), *Consuls of the Later Roman Empire* (Atlanta, Ga., 1987).

BARON, S. W., *A Social and Religious History of the Jews*, iii–iv (New York, 1957).

BLOCKLEY, R. C., *The Fragmentary Classicising Historians of the Later Roman Empire*, 2 vols. (Liverpool, 1981).

BLUMENKRANZ, B., 'Die jüdischen Beweisgründe im Religionsgespräch mit den Christen in den christlich-lateinischen Sonderschriften des 5. bis 11. Jahrhunderts', *ThZ* 4 (1948), 119–47.

—— 'Les Auteurs chrétiens latins du moyen âge sur les juifs et le judaïsme', *REJ* 11 [111] (1951–2), 5–61.

—— 'Altercatio Aecclesie contra Synagogam. Texte inédit du X^e siècle', *Revue du moyen âge latin*, 10 (1954), 1– 160.

BLUMENKRANZ, B., *Juifs et chrétiens dans le monde occidental 430–1096* (Paris, 1960).

—— *Les Auteurs chrétiens latins du moyen âge sur les juifs et le judaïsme* (Paris, 1963).

—— *Die Judenpredigt Augustins* (Paris, 1946).

—— 'Augustin et les juifs, Augustin et le judaïsme', in id., *Juifs et chrétiens, patristique et moyen âge* (Variorum Reprints, London, 1977), III.

—— 'Juden und Jüdische in christlichen Wunderzählungen. Ein unbekanntes Gebiet religiöser Polemik', in id., *Juifs et chrétiens, patristique et moyen âge* (Variorum Reprints, London, 1977), IX.

BONNER, G., *St. Augustine of Hippo: Life and Controversies*[2] (Norwich, 1986).

—— 'Augustine and Millenarianism', in R. Williams (ed.), *The Making of Orthodoxy: Essays in Honour of Henry Chadwick* (Cambridge, 1989), 235–54.

BOUHOT, J.-P., 'Hesychius de Salone et Augustin', in A.-M. la Bonnardière (ed.), *Saint Augustin et la Bible* (Paris, 1986), 229–50.

BOWERS, W. P., 'Jewish Communities in Spain in the Time of Paul the Apostle', *JThS* NS 26 (1975), 395–402.

BRENNAN, B., 'The Conversion of the Jews of Clermont in AD 576', *JThS* NS 36 (1985), 321–35.

BROOTEN, B. J., *Women Leaders in the Ancient Synagogue* (Brown Judaic Studies, 36; Chico, Calif., 1982).

—— 'Jewish Women's History in the Roman Period: A Task for Christian Theology', *Harvard Theological Review*, 1–3 (1986), 22–30.

BROWN, P. R. L., 'St. Augustine's Attitude to Religious Coercion', *JRS* 54 (1964), 107–16.

—— *The Cult of the Saints* (Chicago, 1981).

BURY, J. B., *History of the Later Roman Empire*, 2 vols. (New York, 1958).

CAUBET ITURBE, F. J., '*Et sic omnis Israel salvus fieret*, Rom. 11, 26. Su interpretación por los escritores cristianos de los siglos III–XII', *Estudios biblicos*, 21 (1962), 127–50.

CHADWICK, H., *Priscillian of Avila* (Oxford, 1976).

—— 'Oracles of the End in the Conflict of Paganism and Christianity in the Fourth Century', in E. Lucchesi and H. D. Saffrey (edd.), *Mémorial André-Jean Festugière: Antiquité païenne et chrétienne* (Geneva, 1984), 125–29.

CLARK, E. A., 'Claims on the Bones of Saint Stephen: The Partisans of Melania and Eudocia', *ChHist* 51 (1982), 141–56.

CLOSA FARRES, J., 'Sermo Punicus, sermo Graecus, sermo Latinus y

sermo gentilis en la carta encíclica del obispo Severo de Menorca',
*Helmantica*, 29 (1978), 187–94.

Cohen, J., 'Roman Imperial Policy Toward the Jews from Constantine until the End of the Palestinian Patriarchate (ca. 429)',
*ByzStud* 3 (1976), 1–29.

Cohen, M., 'Severus' Epistle on the Jews: Outline on a New Perspective', *Helmantica*, 106 (1984), 71–9.

Cohen, S. J. D., 'Epigraphical Rabbis', *JQR* 72 (1981), 1–17.

Colafemmina, C., 'Archeologia ed epigrafia ebraica nell'Italia meridionale', in *Italia Judaica: Atti del I convegno internazionale, Bari 18–22 maggio 1981* (Bari, 1983), 199–211.

Collins, R., *Early Medieval Spain* (New York, 1983).

Colorni, V., 'L'uso del greco nella liturgia del guidaismo ellenistico e la novella 146 di Giustiniano', *Annali di storia del diritto*, 8 (1964), 19–80.

Corsini, E., *Introduzione alle 'Storie' de Orosio* (Turin, 1968).

Courcelle, P., 'Propos antichrétiens rapportés par Saint Augustin', *Recherches augustiniennes*, 1 (1958), 149–86.

—— *Histoire littéraire des grandes invasions germaniques* (Paris, 1964).

Cracco Ruggini, L., 'Ebrei e orientali nell'Italia settentrionale fra il IV e il VI secolo d. Cr.', *SDHI* 25 (1959), 186–285.

—— 'Note sugli ebrei in Italia dal IV al XVI secolo', *Rivista Storica Italiana*, 17 (1964), 926–56.

—— 'Pagani, ebrei e cristiani: Odio sociologico e odio teologico nel mondo antico', in *Gli ebrei nell'alto medioevo*, i (Settimane di Studio del Centro Italiano di Studi sull'Alto Medioevo 26, 30 marzo–5 aprile 1978; Spoleto, 1980), 15–117.

—— 'Ebrei e romani a confronto nell'Italia tardoantica', in *Italia Judaica: Atti del I convegno internazionale, Bari 18–22 maggio 1981* (Bari, 1983), 38–65.

—— 'Tolleranza e intolleranza nella società tardoantica: Il caso degli ebrei', *Ricerche di storia sociale e religiosa*, 23 (1983), 27–44.

—— 'Intolerance: Equal and Less Equal in the Roman World', *CPhil* 82 (1987), 187–205.

Curchin, L. A., *Roman Spain: Conquest and Assimilation* (London, 1991).

Daniélou, J., 'La Typologie millénariste de la semaine dans le christianisme primitif', *VChr* 2 (1948), 1–16.

Delehaye, H., 'Les Premiers "libelli miraculorum"', *AnalBoll* 29 (1910), 427–34.

—— 'Les Recueils antiques des miracles des saints', *AnalBoll* 43 (1925), 74–85.

—— *Les Origines du culte des martyrs*² (Brussels, 1980).

DEMOUGEOT, E., 'L'Empereur Honorius et la politique antijuive', in *Hommages à L. Herrmann* (Collection Latomus, 44; Brussels, 1960), 277–91.

—— 'L'Évêque Sévère et les juifs de Minorque au Vᵉ siècle', in *Majorque, Languedoc et Roussillon de l'Antiquité à nos jours* (Montpellier, 1982), 13–34.

DIAZ Y DIAZ, M. C., 'De patrística española', *Revista española de teología*, 17 (1957), 3–46.

DUVAL, Y., *Loca Sanctorum Africae: Le Culte des martyrs en Afrique du IVᵉ au VIIᵉ siècle*, 2 vols. (Rome, 1982).

VAN ESBROECK, M., 'Jean II de Jérusalem et les cultes de S. Étienne, de la Sainte-Sion et de la Croix', *AnalBoll* 102 (1984), 99–134.

FABBRINI, P., *Paolo Orosio, uno storico* (Rome, 1979).

FELDMAN, L. H., *Jew and Gentile in the Ancient World: Attitudes and Interactions from Alexander to Justinian* (Princeton, 1992).

FOLLIET, G., 'La Typologie du *sabbat* chez Saint Augustin. Son interprétation millénariste entre 389 et 400', *REAug* 2 (1956), 371–90.

FREDRIKSEN, P., 'Apocalypse and Redemption in Early Christianity from John of Patmos to Augustine of Hippo', *VChr* 45 (1991), 151–83.

FREND, W. H. C., 'The North African Cult of Martyrs', *Jahrbuch für Antike und Christentum*, 9 (1988), 154–67.

—— 'Augustine and Orosius on the End of the Ancient World', *AugStud* 20 (1989), 1–38.

GARCIA IGLESIAS, L., *Los judios en la España antigua* (Madrid, 1978).

GARCÍA, L. P., *The Balearic Islands* (New York, 1972).

GINZBURG, C., 'La conversione degli ebrei di Minorca (417–418)', *Quaderni storici*, 79 (1992), 277–89.

*Gli Ebrei nell'alto medioevo*, i (Settimane di Studio del Centro Italiano de Studi sull'Alto Medioevo, 26, 30 marzo–5 aprile 1978; Spoleto, 1980).

GOFFART, W., 'The Conversions of Avitus of Clermont, and Similar Passages in Gregory of Tours', in J. Neusner and E. S. Frerichs (edd.), *'To See Ourselves as Others See Us': Christians, Jews, and 'Others' in Late Antiquity* (Chico, Calif., 1985), 473–97.

GUTMANN, J. (ed.), *Ancient Synagogues: The State of Research* (Brown Judaic Studies, 22; Chico, Calif., 1981).

HARKINS, P. W., *Saint John Chrysostom, Discourses against Judaizing Christians* (The Fathers of the Church, 68; Washington, D.C., 1979).

HEFELE, C. J., and LECLERCQ, H. (edd.), *Histoire des Conciles*, 11 vols. (Paris, 1907).

HILLGARTH, J. N., 'Popular Religion in Visigothic Spain', in E. James (ed.), *Visigothic Spain: New Approaches* (Oxford, 1980), 3–60.

HOLUM, K. G., and VIKAN, G., 'The Trier Ivory, *Adventus* Ceremonial, and the Relics of St. Stephen', *DOP* 33 (1979), 113–33.

HORSLEY, G. H. R., 'Name Change as an Indication of Religious Conversion in Antiquity', *Numen*, 34 (1987), 1–17.

—— *New Documents Illustrating Early Christianity: A Review of the Greek Inscriptions and Papyri published in 1979* (Marrickville, N.S.W., 1987).

HUBAUX, J., 'Saint Augustin et la crise cyclique', in id. (ed.), *Augustinus Magister*, vol. 2 (Congrès international augustinien, Paris 21–24 septembre 1954; Paris, 1954), 943–50.

—— 'Saint Augustin et la crise eschatologique de la fin du IV$^e$ siècle', *BAB* 40 (1954), 658–73.

HUNT, E. D., 'St. Stephen in Minorca: An Episode in Jewish–Christian Relations in the Early 5th Century AD', *JThS* NS 33 (1982), 106–23.

—— *Holy Land Pilgrimage in the Later Roman Empire, AD 312–460* (Oxford, 1982).

JACQUES, F., 'Le Défenseur de cité d'après la Lettre 22* de Saint Augustin', *REAug* 32 (1986), 56–73.

JAMES, E. (ed.), *Visigothic Spain: New Approaches* (Oxford, 1980).

JUSTER, J., *Les Juifs dans l'empire romain*, 2 vols. (Paris, 1914).

—— and RABELLO, A. M., 'The Legal Condition of the Jews under the Visigothic Kings', *Israel Law Review*, 11 (1976), 259–87.

KEAY, S. J., *Roman Spain* (London, 1988).

KÖTTING, B., 'Endzeitprognosen zwischen Lactantius und Augustinus', *HJ* 77 (1958), 125–39.

KRAABEL, A. T., 'The Diaspora Synagogue: Archaeological and Epigraphic Evidence since Sukenik', in *ANRW* 19 (1979), 477–510.

KRAEMER, R. S., 'A New Inscription from Malta and the Question of Women Elders in the Diaspora Jewish Communities', *HTR* 78 (1985), 431–8.

—— 'Hellenistic Jewish Women: The Epigraphical Evidence', in K. Richards (ed.), *Society of Biblical Literature Seminar Papers* 25 (Atlanta, 1986), 183–200.

—— 'On the Meaning of the Term "Jew" in Greco-Roman Inscriptions', *Harvard Theological Review*, 82 (1989), 35–53.

—— 'Jewish Women in the Diaspora World of Late Antiquity', in J. R. Baskin (ed.), *Jewish Women in Historical Perspective* (Detroit, 1991), 43–67.

—— *Her Share of the Blessings: Women's Religions Among Pagans, Jews, and Christians in the Greco-Roman World* (New York, 1992).

KRAUSS, S., 'The Jews in the Works of the Church Fathers', *The Jewish Quarterly Review*, 5 (1893), 122–57; 6 (1894), 82–99, 225–61.

LA BONNARDIÈRE, A.-M. (ed.), *Saint Augustin et la Bible* (Paris, 1986).

Lacroix, B., *Orose et ses idées* (Montreal, 1965).

LAFUENTE HERNANDEZ, E., *Epistola Severi episcopi. Edición paleográfica y transcripción latina seguidas de las versiones castellana y catalan de su texto* (Minorca, 1981).

LAGRANGE, M.-J., *Saint Étienne et son sanctuaire à Jérusalem* (Paris, 1894).

LAMBOT, C., 'Les Sermons de Saint Augustin pour les fêtes des martyrs', *AnalBoll* 67 (1949), 249–66.

LANDES, R., 'Lest the Millennium be Fulfilled: Apocalyptic Expectations and the Pattern of Western Chronography 100–800 CE', in W. Verbeke, D. Verhelst, and A. Welkenhuysen (edd.), *The Use and the Abuse of Eschatology in the Middle Ages* (Louvain, 1988), 137–211.

LEON, H. J., *The Jews of Ancient Rome* (Philadelphia, 1960).

LEVINE, L. I., *Ancient Synagogues Revealed* (Detroit, 1982).

—— (ed.), *The Synagogue in Late Antiquity* (Philadelphia, 1987).

LIEU, J., NORTH, J., and RAJAK, T. (edd.), *The Jews Among Pagans and Christians in the Roman Empire* (London, 1992).

LIFSHITZ, B., *Donateurs et fondateurs dans les synagogues juives* (Paris, 1967).

LINDER, A. (ed.), *The Jews in Roman Imperial Legislation* (Detroit, 1987).

LOTTER, F., 'The Forced Conversion of the Jewish Community of Minorca in 418 CE', in *Ninth World Congress of Jewish Studies*, ix (Jerusalem, 1985), 23–37.

MARKUS, R. A., *Saeculum: History and Society in the Theology of St. Augustine* (Cambridge, 1970).

MARROU, H. I., 'Saint Augustin, Orose et l'augustinisme historique', in *La storiografia altomedievale*, i (Settimane di Studio del Centro Italiano di Studi sull' Alto Medioevo 17, Spoleto, 1970), 59–87.

MARTI, H., 'Citations de Térence: Problèmes et significations des exemples de la Lettre 12* de Consentius à Augustin', in C. Lepelley (ed.), *Les Lettres de Saint Augustin découvertes par Johannes Divjak* (Paris, 1983), 243–9.

MARTIN, J., 'Die Revelatio S. Stephani und Verwandtes', *HJ* 77 (1958), 419–33.

MEEKS, W., and WILKEN, R., *Jews and Christians in Antioch in the First Four Centuries of the Common Era* (Missoula, Mont., 1978).

MILLAR, F., 'The Jews of the Graeco-Roman Diaspora between Paganism and Christianity, AD 312–438', in J. Lieu, J. North, and T. Rajak (edd.), *The Jews Among Pagans and Christians in the Roman Empire* (London, 1992), 97–123.

MOMMSEN, T. E., 'Orosius and Augustine', in E. F. Rice (ed.), *Medieval and Renaissance Studies* (Ithaca, NY, 1959), 325–48.

MOREAU, M., 'Lecture de la Lettre 11\* de Consentius à Augustin', in *Les Lettres de Saint Augustin découvertes par Johannes Divjak, communications présentées au colloque des 20 et 21 septembre 1981* (Paris, 1983), 215–23.

MUSSET, L., *The Germanic Invasions* (University Park, Penn., 1975).

PALOL, P. DE, *Arqueologia cristiana de la España romana. Siglos IV–VI* (Madrid, 1967).

PARKES, J., *The Conflict Between the Church and the Synagogue* (Cambridge, 1934).

PASCHOUD, F., *Roma Aeterna: Etudes sur le patriotisme romain dans l'occident latin à l'époque des grandes invasions* (Rome, 1967).

—— 'La polemica provvidenzialistica di Orosio', in id. (ed.), *La storiografia ecclesiastica nella tarda antichità* (Atti del convegno tenuto in Erice, 3–8 dicembre 1978; Messina, 1980), 113–33.

—— 'L'Intolérance chrétienne vue et jugée par les païens', *Cristianesimo nella storia*, 11 (1990), 545–77.

PAUCKER, C., 'De latinitate scriptorum quorundam saeculi quarti et ineuntis quinti p. C. minorum observationes', *Zeitschrift für die österreichischen Gymnasien*, 32 (1881) 481–99.

PEETERS, P., 'Le Sanctuaire de la lapidation de S. Étienne', *AnalBoll* 27 (1908) 359–68.

PERICOT GARCÍA, L., *The Balearic Islands* (New York, 1972).

PHARR, C. (ed.), *The Theodosian Code and Novels and the Sirmondian Constitutions* (Princeton, 1952).

RABELLO, A. M., 'L'Observance des fêtes juives dans l'empire romain', in *ANRW* 19. 1 (1980), 1288–312.

—— 'The Legal Condition of the Jews in the Roman Empire', in *ANRW* 13 (1980), 713–16.

REYNOLDS, J., and TANNENBAUM, R., *Jews and Godfearers at Aphrodisias* (Cambridge Philological Society Supplementary, 12; Cambridge, 1987).

ROUECHÉ, C., 'A New Inscription from Aphrodisias and the Title πατὴρ τῆς πόλεως', *GRBS* 20 (1979), 173–85.

ROUGÉ, J., 'La Navigation hivernale sous l'empire romain', *REA* 54 (1952), 316–25.

SAFRAI, S., 'Education and the Study of the Torah', in *CRINT* 2. 945–70.

—— 'Relations between the Diaspora and the Land of Israel', in *CRINT* 1. 184–215.

SAXER, V., *Morts, martyrs, reliques en Afrique chrétienne aux premiers siècles* (Paris, 1980).

SCHÜRER, E., *The History of the Jewish People in the Age of Jesus Christ (175 B.C.–A.D. 135)*, 3 vols., revised and edited by G. Vermes and F. Millar (Edinburgh, 1973–87).

SEGUÍ VIDAL, G. (ed.), *La carta-encíclica del obispo Severo. Estudio crítico de su autenticidad e integridad con un bosqujo histórico del cristianismo balear anterior al s. VIII* (Palma de Majorca, 1937).

SEGUÍ VIDAL, G., and HILLGARTH, J. N., *La 'Altercatio' y la basilica paleocristiana de Son Bou de Menorca* (Palma de Majorca, 1955).

SIMON, M., *St. Stephen and the Hellenists in the Primitive Church* (London, New York, and Toronto, 1958).

—— 'La Polémique antijuive de saint Jean Chrysostome et le mouvement judaïsant d'Antioche', in id., *Recherches d'Histoire Judéo-Chrétienne* (Paris, 1962), 140–53.

—— *Verus Israel: A Study of the Relations between Christians and Jews in the Roman Empire (135–425)* (Eng. tr.: New York, 1986).

SOTOMAYOR Y MURO, M., 'La iglesia en la España romana', in R. G. Villoslada, M. Sotomayor y Muro, T. Gonzalez Garcia, *et al.* (edd.), *Historia de la Iglesia en España*, i: *La iglesia en la España romana y visigoda* (Madrid, 1979), 355–65.

THOMPSON, E. A., 'The Settlement of the Barbarians in Southern Gaul', *JRS* 46 (1956), 65–75.

—— 'The Conversion of the Visigoths to Catholicism', *Nottingham Medieval Studies*, 4 (1960), 4–35.

—— 'The End of Roman Spain, Part I', *Nottingham Medieval Studies*, 20 (1976), 3–28.

—— 'The End of Roman Spain, Part II', *Nottingham Medieval Studies*, 21 (1977), 3–31.

VAN DAM, R., '"Sheep in Wolves' Clothing": The Letters of Consentius to Augustine', *JEH* 37 (1986), 515–35.

VAN DER MEER, F., *Augustine the Bishop* (London, 1961).

VANDERLINDEN, S., 'Revelatio Sancti Stephani', *REByz* 4 (1946) 178–217.

VENY, C., *Corpus de las inscripciones balearicas hasta la dominacion arabe* (Rome, 1965).

—— 'Early Christianity in the Balearic Islands', *Classical Folia*, 21 (1967) 210–23.

*Vie des saints et des bienheureux selon l'ordre du calendrier avec l'historique des fêtes*, 12 vols. (Paris, 1956).

WANKENNE, J., 'La Correspondance de Consentius avec Saint Augustin', in C. Lepelley (ed.), *Les Lettres de Saint Augustin découvertes par Johannes Divjak* (Paris, 1982), 225–42.

WANKENNE, J., and HAMBENNE, B., 'La Lettre-encyclique de Severus évêque de Minorque au début du Vᵉ siècle', *Revue bénédictine*, 97 (1987), 13–27.

WHELPTON, E., *The Balearics: Majorca, Minorca, Ibiza* (London, 1956).

WILKEN, R. L., *Judaism and the Early Christian Mind* (New Haven, 1971).

—— *John Chrysostom and the Jews: Rhetoric and Reality in the Late 4th Century* (Berkeley, Calif., 1983).

WILLIAMS, A. LUKYN, *Adversus Judaeos* (Cambridge, 1935).

# INDEX

## DATE DUE

| | | | |
|---|---|---|---|
| | | | |
| | | | |
| | | | |
| | | | |
| | | | |
| | | | |
| | | | |
| | | | |
| | | | |
| | | | |
| | | | |
| | | | |
| | | | |
| | | | |
| | | | |
| | | | |
| | | | |
| | | | |
| | | | |
| | | | |